The Blame Game

The Blame Game
Injuries, Insurance, and Injustice

by

JEFFREY O'CONNELL

C. BRIAN KELLY

Lexington Books

D.C. Heath and Company • Lexington, Massachusetts • Toronto

Library of Congress Cataloging-in-Publication Data

O'Connell, Jeffrey.
The blame game.

Includes index.
1. Personal injuries—United States. 2. Liability (Law)—United States. 3. Insurance law—United States. 4. Adversary system (Law)—United States. I. Kelly, C. Brian. II. Title.
KF1257.O26   1987   346.7303'23   86-15294
    ISBN 0-669-11129-5   347.306323
        ISBN 0-669-13916-5 (pbk.)

Copyright © 1987 by D.C. Heath and Company

All rights reserved. No part of this publication may be reproduced or transmitted in any form or by any means, electronic or mechanical, including photocopy, recording, or any information storage or retrieval system, without permission in writing from the publisher.

Published simultaneously in Canada
Printed in the United States of America
Casebound International Standard Book Number: 0-669-11129-5
Paperbound International Standard Book Number: 0-669-13916-5
Library of Congress Catalog Card Number: 86-15294

The paper used in this publication meets the minimum requirements of American National Standard for Information Sciences—Permanence of Paper for Printed Library Materials, ANSI Z39.48-1984.

86 87 88 89 90 8 7 6 5 4 3 2 1

To
Virginia

Contents

	Acknowledgments	ix
	Introduction	xi
1.	Risky Games — Before and After Injury	1
2.	Unsettling Settlements	13
3.	(Mis)Trial by Jury	23
4.	Expert Confusion	33
5.	The Litigation Lottery	43
6.	From Wrecks to Riches	57
7.	The Injured Citizenry	73
8.	Medical Malpractice's Malpractice	85
9.	When Goods Go Bad	97
10.	Reforming Reforms	107
11.	No Fault, No Fee	113
12.	Neo-No-Fault	123
	Appendix	141
	Notes	145
	Index	155
	About the Authors	161

Acknowledgments

WE are grateful to former and present University of Virginia law students and research assistants John Rice, Charles Tenser, and especially James Guinivan; special mention in that category should also be made of Keith Carpenter and Peter Spiro for their valuable help with chapters 3 and 11, respectively. We are also grateful to Charles Peters and Timothy Noah of the *Washington Monthly* for their expert editorial help with chapter 11, portions of which originally appeared in that publication. Chapter 11 also draws on joint writing in the *Virginia Law Review* of Jeffrey O'Connell and Robert Joost, Esq., of Washington, D.C. A lengthy interview, graciously granted, with Seattle attorney Doug McBroom and his paralegal assistant Virginia Towse was the basis of much of chapter 1. Ideas for legislative reform in chapter 12 benefited from consultations with John Hoff, Esq., of Washington, D.C.

Although chapters 1 through 9 result from the joint efforts of the authors, chapters 10 through 12 are the work of Jeffrey O'Connell, drawing in turn on his law review writings cited in the notes to chapters 11 and 12.

Introduction

INJURIES resulting from medical malpractice, defective products, and automobile accidents can lead to dramatic courtroom battles as exciting and confrontational as criminal trials. But such litigation, to say nothing of the personal trauma involved, also leads to wild fluctuations in insurance payments, huge legal costs, and long delays before settlements or verdicts are reached. The whole system is blamed for skyrocketing insurance costs. The result is widespread alarm and cries for reform of tort law throughout the United States.

Perception of the legal system as a game of chance rather than as a sound mechanism for catching unreasonable behavior undercuts the system's ability to raise standards of conduct and deter injuries. Providers of goods and services believe that the legal system itself lacks the capacity to be reasonable and often penalizes only the spurious appearance of fault.

The system's haphazardness also diminishes its value as a protection for the injured. One seriously injured party may recover nothing at all or far less than fair compensation, while another similarly injured receives an award far in excess of his actual loss. Inconsistency is enhanced by allowing juries to award damages for such noneconomic losses as pain and suffering and grief. Because monetary valuation of such nonmonetary losses is inherently irrational, plaintiffs are encouraged to play upon the jury's sympathy, further distorting the issue of who or what was really at fault.

Litigation actually occurs with respect to only a small fraction of claims. Nevertheless, the prospect of litigation determines assessments of settlement possibilities by both defendants and plaintiffs—so huge costs and delays are incurred in evaluating claims, whether they get to court or not. An optimal system would be one that facilitates settlement of most claims by prompt, periodic payment of the injured party's actual economic loss. Yet, the unpredictable and intensely adversarial nature of suits makes such settlements rare today. As one plaintiff's lawyer put it after six years of legal battle before settlement of a complex liability case, "This type of litigation is war—shin-kicking litigation. It often lasts for a long time."[1]

In the following pages, we draw on dramatic cases to examine how the present system actually treats both claimants and defendants. We also consider some highly controversial reforms of the legal system now being debated in Congress and in every state, and then present our own proposals for change. We envision changes in the law that would pay injured persons promptly and in a more predictable way for their actual economic losses and thus avoid the delays, uncertainties, and emotional strain of protracted legal battle.

1

Risky Games—
Before and After Injury

AT age 15, Chris Thompson was six foot one, a sophomore in high school, and a varsity fullback. He and his mother, Louisa Ann—a divorced psychologist who worked for the Seattle public school system—lived a life far removed from that of Seattle attorney Doug McBroom, a personal injury specialist. In mid-1975, none of the three possibly could have foreseen that their lives would soon converge and that they would share in a years-long ordeal dictated by a blind form of cruelty.

Chris had been honored as the best all-around athlete at his junior high school—and no wonder. He played football, he played baseball and basketball, he played golf, he played tennis. In one memorable weekend, he played seven different sports. He was, in short, a physical marvel.

Early in the fall of 1975, his West Seattle football team journeyed to nearby Renton, Washington, to play Lindbergh High School. Both were varsity teams that played a competitive brand of football. Still, it appeared to be just another game.

Once the opening whistle blew, however, players and fans alike could see it was more than "just another game." The onlookers' interest grew shortly before the half, when young Chris Thompson took a swing pass in his own backfield, broke one tackle, and turned the corner with a lot of daylight ahead. The large opening was temporary, however, as Lindbergh's defensive players fought off their blocks and pursued laterally—"cutting down the angle" as their coaches had taught them. Thompson lowered his head and collided with his opponents, in one of the countless collisions that week in football. But this time something was wrong—as the pileup of players cleared, Thompson failed to get up. The collision had caused his spinal cord to snap.

The resulting injury left the handsome teenager a quadriplegic. From then on, his life would be conducted from a wheelchair. For Chris, his mother, and others yet to be drawn into the stark situation, it obviously had not been "just another game." A still-growing, extraordinarily coordinated boy had lost his basic mobility for a lifetime.

Coupled with the physical and emotional wounds was a horrendous monetary cost. The costs of medical care and rehabilitation for Chris far exceeded his mother's budget, and her attempts to find a way to pay the bills proved to be a long and painful ordeal for herself, for Chris, and for others to whom she turned for succor.

At first, Louisa Ann ("Lou") Thompson was unable to find a lawyer interested in her son's potential liability case. By the time she found her way to Doug McBroom's office, four or five attorneys had turned her down, and time was running out. It was June 1978, and the statute of limitations for Chris's injury on the football field nearly three years before was close to running out, an expiration which would preclude any lawsuit seeking damages.

Struck by Lou's energy and her dedication to her son's cause, McBroom was definitely intrigued, but at first, he didn't see a convincing theory on which to base a suit. He agreed to take the case but took some time to look into the facts. On September 19, 1978, the day before the statute of limitations would run out, he filed suit.

In addition to the Seattle School District, the suit sought redress for Chris Thompson's injury from the Renton School District, the Washington Interscholastic Athletic Association (WIAA), and the makers of the young athlete's football helmet. Altogether, Chris and his mother were seeking $7.5 million in damages.

Now came the real work for McBroom and his legal assistant—collecting and reading the literature on similar cases, lining up witnesses, studying the appropriate law, viewing the Renton game films again and again, swatting back at a swarm of defense motions, and dealing with the young plaintiff's single-minded mother.

The trial date had been set for April 1981. By November 1980, McBroom had done an enormous amount of work on the case but still lacked a really compelling theory of liability to carry into King County Superior Court. By then, too, the cost of the apparently uncertain case was mounting up for McBroom's law firm. His partners urged him to drop it, but he insisted on proceeding—the case was "beginning to crawl over me like ants."

McBroom managed to win a continuance until January 1982 and continued his search for the liability "link" somewhere in the volumes of material that filled an entire bookcase in his office. McBroom ordered a set of still prints from the films of the fateful game and studied them one by one, again and again.

Finally, McBroom noticed that Chris had lowered his head just before he was tackled—a critical mistake. But had the youngster been drilled in football practice sessions against that mistake? McBroom, who thought not, at last had his theory.

But he had problems, too. For one, Chris's mother, Lou, was both anxious and impatient. "Chris and I got to be very close," explains McBroom. "He was like my younger brother. His mother [on the other hand] was a plaintiff who couldn't stay out of the case." Generally, McBroom encourages his clients to participate in their cases, to air all their own ideas, but Lou was an extremist in that regard. She had many theories of liability to propose, but she reacted sharply against any that seemed to imply that the injury was her son's fault in any way. Strategy "discussions," says McBroom, often were so intense that he and Lou wound up screaming obscenities at each other. At one point, he remembers, he shouted, "Why don't you try your own case!"

By mid-1981, the case had drained so much of the law firm's resources that McBroom's partners told him he would have to pay future expenses out of his own pocket—no more staff time could be spent on so uncertain a cause of action.

At that point, Virginia Towse—Chris's high school girlfriend and, since 1979, his attendant—became more than simply a supportive onlooker. Virginia went to work for McBroom, being paid $500 a month by Lou Thompson. At about the same time, the helmet manufacturer had agreed to a $95,000 settlement, which covered the mounting expenses (overall, about $90,000 was spent in preparing the case), and the Renton School District settled for another $25,000.

When Virginia first began reporting to work at McBroom's office in June 1981, it was a frenzied time, with the various defendants constantly filing new motions. "The lawyers really came after us with motions and other harassing tactics," says the tall, bespectacled McBroom. Worse yet, he notes, the judge thought the case was worthless.

Initially, McBroom couldn't find expert witnesses willing to testify for his side. No local people involved in sports medicine wanted any part of a suit against the public schools. And McBroom faced deadlines for filing lists of potential witnesses as part of the mutual discovery process for both sides in the case. Virginia, poring through library references, at last came across a monograph that discussed the need for practice drills to prevent the kind of injury Chris had suffered. Unfortunately, in another seemingly typical setback, the author of the monograph was on vacation and couldn't be located. He later was found, however, and agreed to testify.

Another problem was Chris's football coach, Paul Quam. Not that there was anything wrong with him—in fact, he was extremely popular among the followers and players of high school football in Seattle, and he probably was the most safety-conscious coach in the city. He had even written a thesis on the safety of football helmets and had experimented with padding to make them safer. Quam was extraordinarily sensitive to the safety of his players; for example, before the Renton game, he had taken Chris to a special treatment center for attention to a strained muscle. How, McBroom wondered, can you attack a guy like that?

A deposition taken from Quam turned out to be disappointingly vague, and the plaintiffs then had to search out drill sheets for 1975—the year of Chris's injury, six years before.

In the meantime, another problem involved the part to be played by Chris's football teammates. As much as they loved Chris—an outstanding youngster in many ways—they also loved their coach. According to McBroom, the other football players were led to believe that Chris was suing Paul Quam, when in fact the school district was the defendant. Virginia, by then a pre-med student in college, spent her evenings talking to Chris's teammates and lining them up as prospective witnesses. But then, says McBroom, they would hear another story from the defense—that the suit could cost Quam his job. The players would turn on McBroom and Virginia with bitter accusations—"You lied to me"—and the task of wooing them would begin all over again.

The theory for including the WIAA as a defendant was its overall supervisory role in high school athletics throughout the state of Washington. This was a tenuous theory, as McBroom freely acknowledges. Still, the WIAA and its library were a fat repository for all the latest in safety literature and films. The material was there for any school personnel who wanted to see it—literature full of safety tips, films with warnings never to lower the head in football or the neck *could* be broken. However, the material was never publicized or disseminated other than in a WIAA handbook, which McBroom considered cursory at best.

Nonetheless, the WIAA eventually was granted a summary judgment removing the organization from the case altogether. This was a plus for McBroom and his clients, because it removed the most active and energetic of the defense attorneys lined up against their personal injury suit. McBroom later realized that the WIAA's leavetaking, an apparent setback at the time, was actually a blessing in disguise.

Money continued to be a problem for the plaintiffs—not only because of the costs of preparing Chris's case. At the same time, McBroom's law firm had spent about $300,000 on another major suit, this one involving lead poisoning among children who lived near a smelter in Idaho. The firm was basically broke; it had a $500,000 bank loan outstanding, and the bank was unwilling to lend any more. The cash flow was so low that the firm could not issue paychecks for the moment, and all five partners, including McBroom, refinanced their homes to weather the shortage in funds.

It was also a difficult period emotionally. Several of McBroom's partners were going through divorces, and he and partner Leonard Schroeter, who was working on the Thompson case with him, were constantly at loggerheads over conduct of the case. While McBroom was busy with the liability issue, Schroeter was supposed to be addressing the question of appropriate damages—but in McBroom's view, he really hadn't done anything. At the time, it appeared to McBroom that all he was doing was harassing and second-guessing, while also sympathizing with the impatient Lou Thompson on what an "incompetent" McBroom was. At that point, McBroom had lined up sixty potential witnesses for his liability contention, and he noticed that the defense attorneys also seemed to be spending their best effort on the liability aspect, rather than on the damages question.

By then, Virginia was putting in ten hours a day on the case, despite the demands of her pre-med regimen. She and/or McBroom had to travel all over the country—she to help gather evidence, he to take depositions as the trial date drew closer and closer—and they had to travel inexpensively whenever possible. At one point, with no sports medicine experts in Seattle willing to testify for Chris, McBroom located an expert in Hobbs, New Mexico. He flew to see him in a two-engine airplane, which almost crashed on the hop from Albuquerque into Hobbs. McBroom's only thought at that moment was, "All the original X-rays are in my briefcase—and they'll be destroyed!"

Back in Seattle, where it seldom snows, it snowed with a vengeance a week before the pending trial date in January 1982. Chris—along with many others in the city—couldn't even leave home.

By this point, McBroom and his helpers had amassed thousands of documents, but the end still came in a rush. The typical piece of evidence for a severely injured plaintiff—a film depicting "a day in the life of" the victim—had to be completed in one day, December 29. The damages portion of the case was not completed until after the trial began. Clearly, though, there was considerable evidence to show the Seattle jury about the damages done to Chris and his future life as a result of his devastating injury. Here was a handsome, articulate, fully developed young man, a superb athlete—in college by the time of the trial and grown to six foot six—who required a $20,000, specially equipped van to drive around, who wore out two or three wheelchairs a year, who was hospitalized several times a year because of his vulnerability to respiratory infections, who had to be turned in his bed every two hours at night, who had no control of his bladder or bowels, whose overall life expectancy was reduced, whose job prospects were grievously handicapped, whose mobility (in a wheelchair) was so limited that, at best, he could make himself a sandwich or turn on the television set in his home.

On the eve of the all-important trial, the strategy arguments among the principals on the plaintiff's side of the case raged on, often bitterly. McBroom's partner, Schroeter, theorized that Lou should testify that she never would have allowed her son to play football if she had really known the dangers entailed. McBroom felt that line of argument was full of holes because of Chris's unusual career as a schoolboy athlete. Indeed, his experience with sports and its concomitant injuries had been considerable. He had begun playing tackle football at age 9 in West Seattle's Midget B League; he was then a running back and a linebacker in Little League football to age 14. Once, when he was 11, he had been knocked unconscious in a game and suffered a concussion. At age 13, a shoulder separation sidelined him for most of the season; he recovered just in time to rejoin his Little League squad for its playoff and championship games at the end of the season. He had sat out the year he was 14 because, by league rules, he was too heavy for his age group. Meanwhile, he took part in track, and played basketball and baseball in junior high school, once again suffering an injury—a hairline break of his left forearm, incurred while playing third base one day. When Chris returned to football in August 1975 at West Seattle High, he was, even as a sophomore, one of the team's larger backs—and a real veteran of organized sports.

Thus, it was McBroom's contention that both Chris and his mother had known there was *some* risk of injury in football; the real issue was whether he had been warned against possible spinal injury as a result of lowering his head as a battering ram against an onrushing opponent. The differences in theory led to a loud shouting match between the two lawyers for the plaintiffs, and Lou was obviously torn between them and their theories of the case. On the eve of trial, just about all communication among the principals seemed to be at the top of their lungs. The pressure was on. If he hadn't known otherwise, McBroom could have guessed from his hives. Before a big case, he always breaks out in hives; this time, he recalls, they were huge.

The pressure only mounted during the trial, which lasted four and a half weeks. Emotionally, it was an affair of sweeping ups and downs. McBroom and his indefatigable assistant, Virginia, lived on junk food, and McBroom found that he was smoking four or five packs of cigarettes a day—even though he couldn't light up when he was in court for many hours at a time. It was also a period of high confrontation between McBroom and Hugh McClure, the defense lawyer representing Hartford Insurance Company, which would have to pay the first $500,000 of any judgment against the Seattle schools. Actually, in pretrial bargaining as late as December 1981, McBroom and his clients would have settled for $500,000, but the defense brushed off any such settlement notions.

As the trial unfolded, McBroom's intent was to show that it was the obligation of Chris's school to devise a safety program for properly instructing its young athletes in how to avoid unwarranted injury. The popular Coach Quam was seated at the defense table throughout—a common tactic to personalize the defense of a case. McBroom called Quam to the stand for two days as an adverse witness. Again and again, Quam and McBroom went through the drills Quam had given his football players to teach them the "right moves" as a matter of instinct on the field. The more Quam testified, McBroom felt, the more his own case began to jell. It seemed clear to McBroom that the drills failed to instruct the players to keep their heads up, except to see where they were going. It appeared the school authorities hadn't really thought of the more specific warning against injury.

When Quam was questioned by the defense lawyers, however, he spoke of drills in which the players *were* appropriately instructed. Suspicious, McBroom on re-direct (similar, in the case of an adverse witness like Quam, to cross-examination) hammered away at the newly mentioned drills. Were they given on this day, he asked, or that day? They hadn't been. The point that McBroom was finally able to make was that these drills had not been conducted in 1975, the year Chris was hurt.

As the trial proceeded, McBroom was also able to hammer home his contention that the schools were far more careful in planning the academic curriculum than in curriculum planning for safety in sports. The attorney noted that Coach Quam was teaching five hours of algebra a day as a result of school budget cuts and thus was overloaded in view of his concurrent coaching responsibilities.

At another point, McBroom felt that he had made mincemeat of a key school official—but he then made the mistake of recalling the same witness the next morning to drive home the telling points. "He murdered me," says McBroom. "I shouldn't have questioned him any further." McBroom couldn't bring himself to eat lunch that day.

At another time, it was Lou who was unusually upset. As a male friend of the family was testifying, it was suggested that he was having an affair with Lou, a single mother raising three boys.

Meanwhile, Lou, as a psychologist and holder of a doctorate who worked for the same school district, kept trying to persuade McBroom to use various statistics in the case. He didn't believe that the statistical evidence she suggested was very convincing; in fact, he didn't quite understand it. Adding to McBroom's tribulations was the pressure from his office to make good—to use this or that tactic—for by now the law firm's very survival could be affected by the outcome of the Chris Thompson case.

The trial lasted from January 11 to February 11, 1982. Toward the end, McBroom was feeling better about the case; he thought it was going well after all, and Chris might win a handsome verdict. On the Friday night of the last weekend during the trial period, Lou and Chris and Virginia, all feeling bouyant, went to a wedding party. They had a wonderful time and stayed out rather late. After they returned home, however, Lou began to feel ill. Before the next day was over, she was in the hospital—the victim of a massive stroke. She was in a coma, and it was clear even then that she would die.

In the courtroom Lou had left behind, two days of rebuttal testimony remained before the case would go to the jury. Chris was called to the stand as a rebuttal witness, but was understandably "flat," says McBroom. The young man's mother lay unconscious in her hospital bed, and Chris now spent most of his waking hours at the hospital, instead of in the court where his six-and-a-half-year-old suit hung in the balance. "You must understand the relationship between Lou and Chris," adds McBroom. "Lou had saved Chris's life—at one point he had tried to kill himself. They were both strong people with a bond of steel between them."

When they were informed of Lou's condition, the jurors were visibly stunned, but Judge Gerard Shellan denied a defense motion for a mistrial. Then, in closing arguments, McBroom's "damages" partner, Leonard

Schroeter, noted that the Thompson suit sought damages for Lou as well as for her son. "She has rights, though she is lying in a hospital dying," said Schroeter. He cited her six years of struggle on behalf of her crippled son, a burden she had accepted willingly. "But this took a terrible toll; she could not relax; her whole life was geared to his survival." As Schroeter put it, "She testified that Chris was the bravest person she had ever known, but her courage matches [that of] her son."[1]

In final arguments, Schroeter also said that an award of the full $7.5 million sought in the Thompson suit "would not address his mother's pain and suffering over the past six and one-half years."[2] He said that Chris's documented medical costs to date came to $85,000, discounting the donation of two specially equipped vans worth $20,000 each. Projected future damages, of course, were greater—$3.5 million in projected loss of earnings over the next forty years, plus the cost of medical and personal care. In addition, Schroeter called for an award of $500,000 for the injured athlete's pain and suffering and another $3.5 million in damages attributed to the youth's reduced life expectancy.

McBroom and defense attorney Hugh McClure argued the basic liability issue in the case, with McBroom asserting that the school district failed to instruct and drill its football players against lowering their heads and McClure depicting the accident as an isolated, "freak" occurrence. In his view, all football players assume some risk, but McBroom zeroed in on what he saw as a different, more specific issue. "Failure to instruct led directly to this tragedy," he contended at one point. "Chris Thompson did this to himself, put himself in maximum danger, [but] did it because he was not coached in any other way."[3]

At one point in the closing arguments, McBroom was heartened to see one of the jurors perceptibly nodding in agreement with adversary lawyer McClure—heartened because McClure was asking rhetorically whether the school district should have instructed its students on the dangers of football every month. The juror was still nodding in affirmation when McClure went on to ask: every week? even every day? The same juror later rolled his eyes in apparent exasperation at other points McClure made.

Now, with Chris constantly at his mother's bedside, the case was finally handed over to the jury—and still there was buzzing activity among the lawyers and their clients. The defense offered a settlement of $600,000. McBroom and Chris carefully reviewed his minimum needs and came up with a counteroffer of $975,000. With 25 percent deducted as attorney's fees, Chris would have over $500,000 and could "survive."

Meanwhile, the jury stirred wild speculation among all the parties by asking for a rerun of the game film. Altogether, the jury had 200 exhibits to consider, and few observers were surprised when the panels' deliberation behind closed doors extended to a second day. McBroom, of course, found the delay racking—"I was in a state of paralysis," he recalls.

Then, at 1 P.M. on the second day of deliberation, the defense offered a settlement of $875,000, just $100,000 less than the plaintiff side's bottom-line proposal. McBroom was racked anew. Even though he felt the case had gone well, he feared the still-lingering risk of an adverse jury verdict. "If I were to send my kid across the street with a one in twenty chance he would get hit by a car, I would never do it no matter what good was to be served by doing it." McBroom's advice was for Chris to accept the latest settlement offer, and Schroeter hurried off to Lou's hospital to convince young Chris. Later in the afternoon, the settlement issue still unresolved, word came that the jury was ready—it had reached a verdict.

The lawyers called Chris to say that he could still take the settlement. Although McBroom had counseled Chris on the advantages of doing so, he had left the final decision up to his young client. "You guys were terrific," Virginia Towse later told him. "You never put any pressure on him to accept or reject the settlement, but left the decision to him."

It was then that McBroom realized that Chris was no longer a "younger brother" but was an adult capable of making his own excruciating choice: As the handicapped young man calmly put it, "Let's go see what the jury does."

What the jury did stunned the defendants, the world of high school football, even Chris Thompson. The jury awarded Chris $6.3 million in damages and his dying mother another $100,000—a total of $6.4 million. "I never thought I'd get this much," Chris confided later, when shaking hands with the jurors. At the moment of the courtroom announcement, the *Seattle Times*[4] noted the next day, Chris turned his wheelchair toward the jury box, smiled broadly, and said, "Thank you." As the newspaper also reported, the jurors had decided very early in their deliberations that the school district was liable. The rest of the panel's time had been spent determining the amount of damages to award. In the end, the jurors deducted about $130,000 or 2 percent of their actual award to Chris, for his contributory negligence in the football accident. That was one reason they had asked to see the game film again—to see if other players were lowering their heads in blocking or tackling situations.

What had made Chris decide to gamble on the jury's verdict? Chris revealed that it was "vibes" from his comatose mother Lou that encouraged him to take his chances with the jury rather than to accept the final settlement offer from the defense. "I was at the hospital with my mom, when I heard about the settlement offer," he said. "I talked to my mom about it, even though she couldn't respond. She couldn't give me any advice, but I could feel the vibes that she wanted me to go with what the jury decided."[5]

Louisa Ann Thompson died the day after that decision was delivered in court.

But Chris still had to face an inevitable appeal from the losing side. Seven years between injury and verdict isn't enough time for the law. (This raises, incidentally, a point about a defense lawyer's function in such a case. He has two jobs. The first is to try to win the case; the second is to try to make sure that even if he loses, there is error in the record, so that the loss will be appealable.) So an appeal was filed, and for many months the case appeared headed for the state's supreme court for further proceedings. For Chris, 22 by then and a student at the University of Washington, his postgraduation plans depended on what happened with the lawsuit.

On the one hand, he told a hometown newspaper, he might end up in law school. But "if I have enough money, I might become a professor of history," he also mused, no longer the kid who innocently took his place in the lineup against Lindbergh High eight years earlier. "I'm not only bitter," he said, "I'm kind of worn out about the whole thing. And there's no end in sight."[6]

Finally, there was. McBroom felt that their case on appeal was "very, very strong," but there also was the ever-lingering element of risk for his client, the gamble of almost any litigation. Some of the evidence McBroom got admitted at the trial, for instance, presented some knotty issues of admissibility. And after all, the trial had taken over a month. A trial judge is only human—and who can do anything so complicated for weeks at a time and not make mistakes, especially with shrewd professionals trying to lure you into mistakes. Once more, it was the issue of "sending your kid across the street with a one in twenty chance he would get hit by a car." A reversal of the case at this point, added McBroom, would have been "the greatest tragedy of my life since my brother's death. I would still be walking the streets if that happened."

It didn't happen. A week before the Supreme Court of Washington was scheduled to hear arguments in the case, in November 1983, the parties settled at last, for $3.9 million. The terms called for an outright payment of $1 million for Chris, plus an annual stipend of $175,000 for the rest of his life—and $1.2 million to McBroom and his law firm.

From autumn 1975 to autumn 1983—it took eight years for the great and common law, "with all deliberate lassitude," to decide whether insurance money was to be paid to a tragically injured boy. Some insurance. Some law.

2

Unsettling Settlements

ANYONE who thinks "the law" is a dry, nine-to-five business for gnomes in pin-striped suits would have been startled in the early morning hours of May 7, 1984, to find a crowd of about fifty attorneys and corporate executives jammed into a federal judge's chambers in Brooklyn, New York, hoisting paper cups filled with champagne. And no wonder. After nearly six years of preliminary legal maneuvering, on the very eve of trial, they just had settled one of the largest, most emotion-wrought personal injury suits of the century—the suit by American veterans of the Vietnam War claiming injury from exposure to the jungle defoliant called Agent Orange.

Although the litigious bent of Americans and their many willing lawyers seems to set one dubious record after another, the Agent Orange compromise stood, at that moment, as the largest product liability settlement in U.S. history—as American law's largest mass-tort settlement ever.

Untold hours of good, solid legal work went ultimately untested, but the settlement spared the courts and the parties to the class action suit—indeed the entire nation—all the expense and trauma of a difficult, surely wrenching trial that would have ground on for many months, and the inevitable multiple appeals that would have continued for years.

As his actions were to demonstrate, Federal District Judge Jack B. Weinstein was determined from the outset to head off the juggernaut trial bearing down upon his Brooklyn courtroom like some kind of runaway train. One reason for settlement that he urged upon the disputing parties was patriotism, love of country. Chances were, too, that a sympathetic jury would side with the aggrieved veterans, although such a plaintiff's verdict could be reversed upon appeal on issues of law. And then what? Who could possibly be the "winner" in such a sequence of events? The defendant chemical firms, damned in court testimony for the harm they had done? The veterans, deprived at the last of any compensation?

The situation seemed to call for judicial creativity in parceling out some benefit to all parties in the case. And in the eyes of many observers and participants, Judge Weinstein masterfully guided the monster suit to a safe stop. Only history can judge how masterfully, of course, for there were some critics, and there was some unhappiness with the terms, especially among the veterans who were not directly privy to the settlement negotiations. Also, there was a mountain of detail to be sorted out later. Still, an exceedingly difficult trial had been avoided. To all appearances, the settlement process had worked. Or had it?

Before we examine the success of that process in the Agent Orange case, however, it is important to note that settlements are not necessarily fortunate for the involved parties. Settlement is often desirable, especially for the side that apparently has the most to lose by gambling on the outcome in court, but settlement does not always turn out fair, square, and uniform, any more than a full-blown trial does in either civil or criminal cases. Even in settlement, there is the legal system's ubiquitous gamble factor, which is based, in turn, on the unpredictable human factor.

Consider, for example, the cases of Gail Kalmowitz and Jimmy Farrell, both of whom were born prematurely and given life-sustaining oxygen but then were quite accidentally condemned to the handicapped life of the blind or near-blind.

Twenty-one years after her premature birth, Gail, almost completely blind, was the plaintiff in a $2 million medical malpractice suit. After days of testimony and legal argument in Brooklyn Superior Court, the jury of five men and one woman finally had her case in its hands. The jurors soon sent word to the clerk of court that they were ready to deliver a verdict on the claim by the Brooklyn baker's daughter. The case was at its most climactic point when, suddenly, the young woman said that she didn't want to hear the verdict. "I want to settle," she cried out. "I don't want to proceed."

In minutes, the case was settled; as compensation for the blindness allegedly caused when Gail was administered too much oxygen as a "preemie," she would receive $165,000. A few minutes later, Gail, a sophomore at Brooklyn College, was in a corridor outside the courtroom weeping. Weeping with her, though, were some of the suddenly dismissed jurors. Her own tears might have been predicted, but what about those of her jurors?

According to the *New York Times*, they were telling her, "You shouldn't have done it. You should have gone all the way. Our hearts were with you."[1]

The jury, it seems, had been about to give Gail an award of $900,000—$735,000 more than the settlement figure. The handicapped young woman managed to be philosophical. "I was afraid I'd lose everything and wind up with nothing," she later explained. "I think I made a wise decision. Everybody said, 'You've got it won.' But I wasn't sure. They said they definitely would have appealed and there's a chance I would have lost it all."[2]

Not long after and just 200 miles away in suburban Montgomery County, Maryland, outside of Washington, D.C., a jury in a similar case had been deliberating for ten hours. Plaintiff Jimmy Farrell, age 6 by the time of his trial in 1976, also had developed the rare disease called RLF (retrolental fibroplasia) as a premature infant. The blind boy and his parents had sued for $3.5 million. Initially, the defendant hospital's attorneys had offered a settlement of $85,000. When trial actually began nearly six years later, the parties still were $400,000 apart in their bargaining. The plaintiff's attorney's were insisting on $650,000, while the defense clung to $250,000 as its top settlement possibility.

Well into the eight-day trial, however, the defense moved up to $425,000 in the bargaining that continued outside the impaneled jury's ken, but the plaintiffs still held out for at least $600,000. The case finally went to the jury, which deliberated late one day and for part of the next morning. Finally, at 11:40 A.M., a knock came from inside the locked door to the jury room. The jurors were ready to decide Jimmy's financial fate. In minutes, the crucial moment of the legal proceedings would be over, though with appeals ever looming. But again, the lawyers for both sides rushed into fresh, frantic bargaining, each team apparently fearing the worst for its side. While the jury waited, they came together in the judge's chambers and in minutes decided on a $500,000 compromise settlement.

By noon, the youngster's jury had been dismissed, just as Gail's had been, but Jimmy and his parents had won half a million dollars, a good deal more than Gail had received in her similar last-minute settlement.

More to the point, though, was the word that quickly spread outside the Maryland courthouse as the attorneys shook hands with the six men and six women comprising young Jimmy's jury—it would have been a "defense verdict." Had the jury been allowed to step up and announce its decision, the defendant hospital and the two doctors who were also sued would have been exonerated. Jimmy would have gone home with nothing.

Obviously, there was wide disparity not only in the settlements achieved by plaintiffs Gail and Jimmy but also in the sentiment of the two juries that considered their look-alike claims. One plaintiff would have won, one would have lost. It could be argued, then, that the disparate last-minute settlements at least gave each of them *something*.

Still, these two cases do suggest that there is something less than satisfactory about settlement, especially settlement reached under emotional pressure when time is short, when the principals are exhausted by the trial process, and when so much, if not "all," appears to be at stake. Indeed, the bargaining that goes on, before and often during trial can be just as harrowing as a trial itself.

Such thoughts must have been on Judge Weinstein's mind when he assumed the celebrated Agent Orange liability case in October 1983 from another trial judge, who was moving up to an appellate court seat. Settlement would not come easily. Even in outline, the dimensions of the case were horrendous: tens of thousands of plaintiff veterans; millions of dollars in claims against seven defendant chemical companies that had taken part in the production of 12 million gallons of the defoliant used in Vietnam from 1965 to 1970—its use halted after reports of miscarriages and abnormal births among Vietnamese women, glaring publicity, and testimony resurrecting all the heartbreak and controversy of the Vietnam War for the country.

The 62-year-old Weinstein convened with the dozens of lawyers in the case and, using time as his first weapon, established the trial date—May 7, 1984—as the immovable object awaiting the irresistible force headed his way. But was it irresistible? With assent from both sides in the case, Weinstein soon named a "special master" to help settle the case out of court. Kenneth R. Feinberg, 38—a Washington attorney who had been raised in Massachusetts and was a former aide to Senator Edward M. Kennedy (D.-Mass.)—was appointed to explore all possible paths to settlement. Over the next three months, reported the *New York Times*, Feinberg developed settlement proposals and various ways to disburse monetary awards equitably among the injured veterans.[3]

It was as late as April 20, 1984, before this behind-the-scenes operative met with representatives of the disputing parties for the first time. At that point, the settlement figures those parties had in mind were $35 million offered by the defendant chemical firms and $600 million demanded on behalf of the veterans—a spread as wide as many a city's annual budget.

Weinstein was not quite finished in his settlement effort with the appointment of Feinberg as one special master. Joining Feinberg were two more special masters, former presidential counsel Leonard Garment and his partner in a Washington law firm, David Shapiro. All three were to contribute their varied expertise in the negotiations between the seven chemical firms on the one side and, in the words of the *National Law Journal*, the "often fractious" team of various attorneys representing unknown thousands of Vietnam veterans and dependents on the other side.[4]

From the beginning, Judge Weinstein said that the case had been lingering too long and that the trial date of May 7, 1984, was absolutely firm. Also, late in 1983, among other early rulings to define the case better, Weinstein certified a plaintiff's class of possibly more than two million Vietnam veterans and family members.

In the scenario later described in the *National Law Journal*, special master Feinberg began work on a memorandum identifying the prime issues in the Agent Orange case and developing a formula to allocate damages among the defendants—later a difficult sticking point. Weinstein himself told the disputing parties that, in his view, a reasonable settlement could lie in the range of $150 million to $250 million. In the meantime, Garment was looking into the federal government's view of its role in the litigation.

Feinberg and Shapiro, the two men meeting the litigants as special masters on April 20, were a study in contrasts. The *National Law Journal* noted:

> Mr. Feinberg cultivates a studious air and the ingratiating ways of one used to the constant give and take of Congress. Mr. Shapiro, by contrast, is a longtime litigator who has elevated bluntness to an art form.[5]

Said one participant in this early stage of negotiation: "Shapiro hammers at guys; he's a plaintiff's antitrust lawyer, wham, bang, swearing at them."[6]

As the two special masters alternatively applied sweet reason or "bellowed" at the opposing attorneys, both sides had good reason to favor a settlement—beyond avoidance of a long, costly, and difficult trial, which was reason enough. According to the *National Law Journal*, Weinstein himself was a veteran of World War II, a "fact that . . . made the plaintiffs confident that they would win a verdict the judge would sustain."[7] Regardless of the accuracy of that prediction, however, there was also the prospect that some of Weinstein's rulings could be reversed on appeal. Furthermore, the appellate route would cost both sides huge sums more in legal expenses. It was a situation wherein any "victories" could be hollow ones, indeed. Imagine the disappointment and probable bitterness among the vets if they were to win on the trial level, only to lose on appeal because of some seemingly obscure point of law. Then, too, such a monetary reprieve for the defendants would hardly make up for the public relations disaster of an adverse verdict in the lower court. Even a win in lower court might not match the damage to the defendants of the heart-rending stories certain to emerge in trial testimony.

Noting such points, the special masters proceeded in the face of the two major problems they soon encountered. The companies that produced Agent Orange under contract to the government argued that the government was now foisting the resultant liability on them alone. Furthermore, who was to say which of the multitudinous Agent Orange claims were valid? "The defendants had no idea, the plaintiffs had no idea," said one source close to the situation. And plaintiffs' attorney Stanley Chesley claimed: "It's the first time I've ever been in a case where it was next to impossible to determine the total number of cases."[8]

For a time, the same could have been said for the number of attorneys representing plaintiffs in the case. At one point, says the *National Law Journal*, "they totaled 900 lawyers with about 11,000 clients."[9] Scattered across the nation, many had signed on after Long Island attorney Victor J. Yannacone, Jr., filed the first class action suit way back in 1979. It is not surprising that such unwieldy numbers made for disagreement and a constant turnover of lawyers associated with the case. In fact, the three attorneys meeting with the special masters in early 1984 were all newcomers; by the *National Law Journal*'s account, none had participated before June 1983.

Even if settlement were achieved, it would be difficult to determine which and how many veterans' claims deserved actual compensation. As another challenge for Feinberg and his two colleagues, the composite defense seemed to say that it would consider a settlement on the order of $150 million—but only if the government paid a large share. The Justice Department, for its part, was stoutly resisting any such notion.

From Leonard Garment's investigation of the possible government role in the case, though, it was ascertained that the Veterans Administration already was providing about $60 million a year for treatment of Vietnam veterans with alleged disability from Agent Orange. The government was adamantly against providing further compensation to the veterans.

A week before the scheduled trial, the plaintiffs told the special masters that the veterans as a group would accept a settlement of $360 million. The defense offer at that time was $100 million; they were $260 million apart. Further maneuvering resulted in a plaintiffs' figure of $250 million by May 3, an offer coupled with a warning that the defense had better consider $150 million as its opening bargaining figure or there would be no more movement. For the defendants, meanwhile, there was an internecine wrangle over an allocation formula—who should pay what, and on what basis.

With the parties apparently very serious about settling but still at odds, special master Shapiro proposed an around-the-clock marathon negotiating session in Weinstein's Brooklyn courthouse—like a last-ditch labor session designed to avert a strike. Weinstein complied with an order requiring a start at 10 A.M. Saturday, May 5, two days before scheduled trial.

In short order, the entire top floor of the federal courthouse on Cadman Plaza was bustling with nearly fifty attorneys and principals. They occupied four courtrooms, several jury rooms, the judges' cafeteria and conference room—even Weinstein's chambers—and the battery of lawyers representing the Vietnam veterans traveled back and forth between the sixth floor of the federal building and their headquarters down the street.

With the principals of the two sides kept separated and the special masters visiting them alternately, the issue for most of the day was one for the defendants—the allocation conundrum, which, of course, could mean a difference in millions for any of them. Since dioxin, a toxic by-product of Agent Orange, was considered the chief culprit in any injuries caused, shouldn't the amount of dioxin in a company's Agent Orange formula be the criterion for damages? Yes, said the firms that used relatively little of the injurious stuff; no, said the others.

The overall share of Agent Orange sales to the government was also an allocation argument that offended some while pleasing others. One defendant, at least, called for sharing the settlement equally.

The defense lawyers and corporate officials trooped before Judge Weinstein group by group to argue their views of the allocation formula. By about 6 P.M. that Saturday, the judge had written out his view of fair shares. He summoned the defendants and read them his proposals. Not surprisingly, there was a great deal of protest. Four of the seven defendants demanded a second airing of their allocation contentions. Close to midnight, however, Weinstein remained unmoved; according to the *National Law Journal*, "He was sticking with his numbers."[10] At first, one defendant balked and refused to accept them—but faced with the possibility of going to trial alone if the other six settled, the holdout backed down. Thus, one major roadblock was removed.

But as Sunday dawned, the defense offer of $100 million still remained far below the plaintiffs' demand for an opening bid of at least $150 million. This meant more work, more negotiating—and the trial was due to start the next day.

Then, about noon on Sunday, the special masters, still shuttling among the batteries of opposing lawyers, announced a breakthrough: the defense had moved up the ladder to $150 million. Now it was the plaintiffs' turn to feel the settlement pressure. The afternoon was spent in an effort to move them down to $200 million. Meanwhile, the *National Law Journal* noted, "whole blackboards [were filled] with the lists of reservations, conditions and exceptions each side had proferred."[11] Symbolically, as the range of troublesome conditions shrank, daylight appeared ready to break for all concerned. Quickly, then, the plaintiffs agreed to a sealing of the allocation data from the public eye; and the defense acceded to the plaintiffs' insistence upon possible trial before a jury if the negotiations should fall through. Still unresolved, though, was a proposal that the settlement fund reimburse the defendants for any losses they might still face in state courts—up to $10 million in all.

And then came the real rub—the interest building up day by day in the proposed settlement fund itself. Until this point, no one had addressed the troublesome issue; now the plaintiffs contended that the fund should accrue interest, while some on the defense team began to argue that they had never meant to include an interest factor—certainly not from the moment of any agreement to establish a settlement fund. Interest on the many millions at issue could amount to millions more in very short time. "It was at that point," reported the *National Law Journal,* "with the defense threatening to back off from what the plaintiffs thought was already agreed to, that Judge Weinstein decided to call both sides into his chambers."[12]

In his second appearance as stern overlord, Weinstein again stated his ample reasons for avoiding trial, which was due to begin with jury selection the very next morning. In meetings lasting until late in the night, he again cited all the uncertainties in anticipating actions either by the jury or by the appeals courts. It was then that he urged settlement for the sake of patriotism, too.

Just after 1 A.M. Monday, the plaintiffs informed Weinstein that they would go as low as $200 million. Thirty minutes later, they were back with a request to address the defendants face to face, one by one, for the first time in the negotiations. By 2 A.M., the plaintiffs were down to $180 million—but only if interest would accrue immediately, from the moment of signed agreement. As it happened, Weinstein was on their side in the interest issue.

The defendants, though accepting the $180 million sum in principle, insisted that interest should begin accumulating only when the settlement was final, months later. As both sides knew, interest pegged to a national prime rate of 12 percent (the applicable rate at the time) would amount to $61,000 a day, or more than half a million in just ten days. But the defense also wanted its $10 million indemnification against future actions in state courts. Defense attorney William Krohley said later that the defense wanted "whatever practical and legal assurances it could [get] that this settlement was it, that it was final."[13]

The round figure of $180 million had not been an easy pill to swallow by itself, even without the interest factor. When the plaintiffs finally moved down to that figure, the special masters warned that it would not hold for long. Weinstein is reported to have warned defense lawyers: "This is it. One hundred and eighty. They will not go for one seventy-nine."[14]

As 2 A.M. approached, only those two issues—interest and the so-called finality issue of future actions in state courts—prevented mutual acceptance of the $180 million. As things turned out, the plaintiffs agreed to finality and the defense conceded to immediate interest accrued, even if it amounted to the estimated $5.5 million before Weinstein could make the settlement final—after public notice and a series of hearings across the country in the months to come.

In essence, the negotiations were over. After the time required to draft and dicker over the language, Weinstein passed among the disputing parties a two-page list of thirteen settlement specifications. With the principals of the marathon negotiations crowded into his chambers, he also broke open and passed around two bottles of champagne.

That was at 3 A.M. Monday; seven hours later, he appeared in his courtroom for the brief announcement that the case was settled, and the jury panel was discharged.

Actually, many matters still remained unresolved. Still to be determined were the criteria for administering and distributing the $180 million and the issue of which plaintiffs' lawyers were to be paid what fees for which services. But the settlement in the Agent Orange case did result in avoidance of a protracted trial with outcomes impossible to predict. "This was a crapshoot," said one lawyer-participant, a suit that was "too dangerous, too open-ended" while also carrying "very, very high stakes."[15]

For those who are intimately involved, however, every case can represent high stakes, every liability suit is a gamble of sorts, and even the obvious remedy of bargaining—settlement—can be an ordeal. Admittedly, because of its scope, the Agent Orange case is an extreme example of the settlement process at work. Admittedly, too, *some* cases resolve themselves far more simply and with less emotional tension, even pain, than the examples presented thus far. Nonetheless, the Agent Orange case provides a unique look backstage at the chaos that often invades the halls of justice in personal injury cases. Is it possible that there could be alternatives to trial or settlement that are both less traumatic for the principals and less costly to society as a whole?

3

(Mis)Trial by Jury

HIGH on the list of favorite "war stories" swapped at any gathering of lawyers are those concerning juries—a mysterious species that can be notoriously pliable or blindly obstinate, depending on the warring attorneys' points of view. Making lasting impressions on these supposedly fickle people is the name of the game—as almost any student of the trial trade knows. Attorney F. Lee Bailey once brought his immensely wealthy client, Patty Hearst, to the courtroom in oversized clothing that would minimize her glamor and render her small and pathetic-looking.

That was a criminal case, but lawyers' legends arise in the civil trade, too—especially in personal liability cases, where the struggle is similarly over the issue of jury sympathy for the client. A mother, at counsel's request, removes her young daughter's glass eye before a jury deliberating the girl's injury; or pins are stuck into a numbed, useless limb of an injury victim appearing for his day in court. In defense of such tricks of the trade, it is insisted that juries are convened for the express purpose of being persuaded by one side or the other. Argument and evidence to that end are the ideal and often the practice, but in many instances, trial lawyers do their best to manipulate emotion as well.

In addition to the colorful lore they provide, manipulative tricks have long been a source of controversy for the legal brotherhood—but they also seem to evoke fond images of the wizened old country lawyer who isn't so sleepy after all and of the sharp city slicker who, even as villain, is adored for his amazing success. In either case, the image reflects individual, more or less "seat-of-the-pants" reactions to the drama of the courtroom. In fact, many such tactics are thought out well in advance of trial; F. Lee Bailey personally accompanied Patty Hearst on a shopping trip to pick her courtroom clothes. In recent years, however, a much more scientific approach has had a startling impact on courtroom strategy. New tricks of the trade include court simulations, studies of jury psychology, and employment of expert witnesses. And as the wizened old country lawyer should note, the new-fangled "scientific" approach can pay off.

In 1980, for instance, when MCI Communications Corporation was preparing its antitrust case against the monolithic American Telephone and Telegraph Company, a last step for the MCI lawyers was to run their case by groups of mock juries hired to sit for three successive nights, as a trial simulation. Elliot Cahn, an attorney and social scientist who advises other lawyers on jury selection and trial tactics, reported the results in the *American Bar Association Journal* of August 1983: "On the first night the mock jurors were reluctant to enforce a key Federal Communications Commission ruling favorable to MCI's case and brought in a verdict for MCI of [only] $100 million."[1]

But that wasn't enough. Using the information they gleaned from their "simulated" jurors, the MCI lawyers honed and sharpened their presentation. By the third night, the mock jurors were untroubled by the FCC ruling. They "awarded" MCI $900 million.

In the real trial that soon followed, the MCI lawyers stuck by their newly learned modifications, and the real-life jury accepted MCI's claim of liability and awarded real damages of $600 million—a sum then "trebled by the court to a whopping $1.8 billion."[2]

Such trial simulation, added Cahn, is the "analogue of the test-marketing campaigns that manufacturers routinely conduct before releasing a product." Therefore, "it is no surprise that corporations were the first parties to embrace the concept of using this kind of 'market research' in the litigation context."[3]

Before the recent advent of simulations, though, there were other innovations that might be placed in the category of social science research. Cahn noted that social science techniques for jury selection were first explored in the trials of left-wing activists in the turbulent early 1970s. Preparation and presentation of cases by *scientific* criteria then followed rather naturally. In the interim, serious study of jury psychology made its weight felt in legal circles in a fair bid to replace, or at least substantially supplement, the wily country lawyer or the fox-faced Mr. Slick of the courtroom.

It would be nice to think that juries understand their job, overcome their prejudices, expertly judge the credibility of witnesses, sift through the evidence, and collectively apply the law to reach fair verdicts. It always *was* nice to think such rosy thoughts, even when, in fact, practice often proved otherwise. But now the social scientists have arrived in force, with the scientific message that the "nice" assumptions of trial practice indeed do not always bear up. Worse, various psychological factors would seem to preclude fair and rational results in the courtroom. For instance, a simulation study discussed in *The Psychology of the Courtroom*, a collection of essays edited by Norbert L. Kerr and Robert M. Bray, noted that an attorney burdened with the weaker side of a case on trial will expend even greater effort in preparing his case. Thus, in court, the two sides of the case may seem more balanced than the facts warrant.

There are also studies suggesting that the last evidence heard is heard best—that such evidence leaves a more lasting impression. But that's only true in presenting evidence. To the extent that a jury is being asked to appraise people, the party going *first* has the greater influence. It seems to follow, then, that in real life, the jury will tend to favor the first view it gets of credibility of a witness or of the character of a principal party.

Although many of the studies discussed in *The Psychology of the Courtroom* concern defendants in criminal cases, they can also arguably be applied to parties in civil suits. Many of the issues studied are substantially the same in both kinds of trials: the adversary system, the effectiveness of juries, the type of observation called for, the reliability of witnesses, and the psychology of judging. Both criminal and personal injury litigation are characterized by emotional appeals. Criminal defendants and personal injury plaintiffs are often lonely, pathetic figures facing large, impersonal institutions—the state in the case of criminal defendants and large institutions or insurance companies in the case of personal injury plaintiffs. Another important similarity is that both kinds of trial often result from sudden, unexpected, and often violent acts or occurrences.[4]

One essay in *The Psychology of the Courtroom* reinforces a good many precepts of the canny courtroom operator of the past. Certain obvious characteristics of a defendant and a victim in a criminal trial (and, arguably, the plaintiff in a civil trial)—such as gender and attractiveness—have an unfair, unscientific influence. In a simulated burglary case, for example, women received shorter sentences than men when both were "attractive," but they received the same treatment when both were unattractive. Thus, in litigation it pays to be attractive (unless that very characteristic played a part in the commission of a wrong, such as fraud). In a similar study, jurors appeared more willing to favor parties of their own race and less willing to favor those of another race. And still another indication gained from psychological research is that juries consider someone of higher socioeconomic station more trustworthy than someone of lower station.

Important in accident litigation, of course, is the issue of eyewitness testimony and information processing. Social scientists have reduced the information processing to four stages: perception, encoding, remembering, and recall.

In the first stage, distortion in perceptual judgment is commonplace. Subjects will overestimate distance and time duration but underestimate the size of filled spaces, such as a room filled with furniture. In one study, eyewitnesses overestimated a suspect's height by eight inches on the average; in another, they overestimated the duration of a film by a factor of three.

Encoding is simply the social scientist's word for taking in facts. Studies show that the more unusual the event or scene, the more likely it is to be absorbed in some detail. To some degree, the same axiom holds as the situation becomes stressful. But at least one study suggests that extraordinary stress damages memory retention; for instance, in proportion to the level of violence and injury suffered, the victim tends to describe the assailant less and less completely.

Certain expectations can also affect the accuracy of the witness's memory. As one classic study has shown, subjects often fail to recall an unexpected phenomenon, such as a *red* ace of spades. "Deeply processed" information comes back on recall more readily than information that is processed in "shallow," mundane fashion. For example, subjects who are asked to look at photographs and judge the faces before them for honesty and likability are more likely to be able later to identify those examined than are persons who are simply asked to determine the gender of those in the photos.

Such encoding can be critical, of course, to testimony in litigation stemming from accidents, which usually occur suddenly, quickly, and without repetition. Almost any onlooker will recall the bang when the cars hit and the dramatic details, such as a door flying open to spill a passenger on the ground. But was the traffic light green or red? Such critical but everyday details are often lost or forgotten.

The next stage in information processing is the related function of remembering. This actual storage of retained, encoded information is also vulnerable to various vicissitudes. As almost any old-school lawyer always knew, the accuracy of witnesses dims with the passage of time. But something called interference also can undermine accuracy. The wise old country lawyer may have sensed this phenomenon, too—if you ask a witness a few misleading questions about the central event before he can testify to it, you may well have diminished his memory of the event itself.

Finally, recall, or the retrieval of stored information, can be affected by the form in which questions are asked. Did the two cars "collide," "hit," "bump," or have "contact"? When combined with the question of how fast the cars were going when they came together, these word choices have been shown to produce significantly varying estimates of the speed involved.

Such issues are important in anticipating a jury's response to eyewitness testimony, to which jurors tend to respond strongly (perhaps too strongly). In one study, for instance, three mock jury groups were exposed to "testimony" about the same armed robbery. One group was given circumstantial evidence implicating the defendant; 19 percent voted to convict. A second group was treated to an "eyewitness" account along with the circumstantial evidence; 72 percent voted to convict. In the third go-around, however, everything was the same as in the second, except that the unfortunate "eyewitness" suffered poor vision and was not wearing glasses at the time of the robbery. The third jury was informed of the handicap but still convicted at a high rate—68 percent.

How are juries expected to spot an unmitigated liar on the stand? Many studies have indicated that jurors are, in fact, surprisingly inept at spotting liars. They tend to look for stereotypical clues to lying. According to communications professors Gerald R. Miller and Judee K. Burgeon of Michigan State University, the witness is in trouble if he demonstrates little eye contact, shows nervousness, is slow to respond to questions, is given to dramatic gesture, uses garbled language, swallows markedly, displays a certain "stiffness," or shows unnatural-appearing smiles, a "tight" face, or such mannerisms as scratching his head. The problem with drawing any conclusions from such restless behavior is that the behavior often results from anxiety or stress associated simply with appearing in a courtroom.

According to the two Michigan State scholars, various studies have shown that average observers "are not very successful in detecting deception perpetuated by relative strangers." In fact, the observers cited in most studies "would probably have done as well had they flipped a coin to determine if the communicator/deceivers were lying." Paradoxically, the subject observers also feel quite confident of their ability to spot the lying witness or the truthful paragon, even when they are absolutely wrong. Miller and Burgeon have noted: "Translated to the courtroom environment, this finding raises the specter of jurors evaluating a witness's veracity inaccurately while remaining very certain of the correctness of their evaluations."

Regarding a juror's bias and its possible effect on his or her verdict, there is evidence that biases are systematically related to general personality traits. For instance, if a favorable attitude toward the death penalty really is linked to personal "dispositions to stringency," reports psychologist Martin

F. Kaplan, a professor at Northern Illinois University, we can expect a tendency to be conservative rather than liberal, authoritarian rather than egalitarian. The resulting attitude would be more pro–law enforcement in a criminal case and, as a corollary, arguably more pro-defendant in a civil suit.

What does all this scientific study mean for the litigation process in general? Do trial lawyers now spend large amounts of time reading up on the latest psychological studies predicting jury behavior? Some probably do, but others have been turning to behavioral consultants in recent years—psychologists, market researchers, and the like, many of whom are in business solely to serve the legal fraternity. As the *Wall Street Journal* has reported: "The behavioral consultants advise on how to select sympathetic jurors and how to use psychological techniques to persuade juries in cases that often take months to try." The primary customers for these consultants are major corporations, "the frequent targets of blockbuster suits."[5]

Not everyone in the legal field is so impressed by the scientific approach, however, "Behavioral consultants are of questionable value," contends Maxwell M. Bleecher of Los Angeles, a prominent plaintiffs' attorney. "They don't offer perspectives much different from those of the experienced trial lawyer."[6] Hans Zeisel, law professor at the University of Chicago and a student of jury behavior, agrees: "At best, these consultants only supplement a good lawyer."[7] But many others disagree or, at the least, concede that the social science approach has an impact. According to David Boies, one of the nation's most successful litigators and partner in a large New York law firm that has used the services of such consultants: "In the past four years, we've seen a large increase in the use of social-science consulting firms, and we'll see a lot more in the future.[8]

In 1977, in one famous case marked by the social science trend, International Business Machines Corporation prepared for a $300 million antitrust suit with a "shadow jury" as one of its major weapons for the pending trial against the plaintiff, California Computer Products Inc. The shadow jury, selected for demographic and psychological traits similar to those of the actual jurors in the case, attended the trial as visitors every day. In the evenings, its members told IBM consultant David E. Vinson their reactions to the day's events.

Former U.S. Attorney General Nicholas Katzenbach, IBM's general counsel at the time, later said that the shadow jury enabled IBM to determine whether its points, often technical, were getting across to the lay jurors. David Boies, participating as lead IBM counsel for the trial, said, "To have that kind of daily feedback was great."[9] With it, he explained, he learned whether he was proceeding too fast or too slowly in presenting his evidence. The comments helped him find the right pace.

After two months, though, the shadow jury's presence was discovered by the press, and the attendant controversy forced Katzenbach to disband the group. For whatever reasons, IBM later won the case by directed verdict, and Vinson, a marketing professor at the University of Southern California, went on to found his own consulting firm, Litigation Sciences.

For their litigation against each other in 1980, both MCI and AT&T hired pollsters to assess public opinion. The proliferating social research consultants say that it can be better to settle a case out of court if such polling discovers the concerned party has a bad image in the community.

In another trend, Litigation Sciences uses a bank of experts, such as psychologists and market researchers, to "profile" prospective jurors and single out favorable or high-risk types. "Insurance companies have become increasingly appreciative of the services of legal consultants who specialize in litigation psychology," wrote Judith Gonda, the firm's research director, in the *National Underwriter*.[10] She also stated: "Behavioral and psychological techniques aid in the selection of more favorable juries, persuading juries to return favorable verdicts, and in the reduction of punitive damages." Thus, during the *voir dire*, in which jurors are selected from the pool at hand, the prospects for jury duty are studied psychologically, and that assessment, together with pretrial study of the demographics of the same venue's previous juries, "provides attorneys with information that is useful in predicting the attitudinal nature of the [forthcoming] jury."[11]

As an example of how the demographics of previous juries can matter, Gonda indicated that a demographic profile would differentiate between a small community that would be receptive to an "outsider" attorney and a small community "where an outsider would be viewed suspiciously and not trusted."[12] Such information could determine whether local attorneys should be hired to handle the case.

According to Gonda, psychological assessment of prospective jurors can be helpful not only in jury selection on *voir dire* but also in choosing trial tactics. The point is to match those tactics with the "attitudinal orientation" of the jurors—a concept known as *selective attention*. But consultants like Gonda also find the special interests of juries rather interesting: "In other words, communications directed to particular subpopulations are more effective than those directed to the general public."[13] An attorney who has studied the makeup of the jury might use subliminal messages: "As all us parents in the room certainly realize . . . " or, more blatantly, "My fellow Texans, . . ." The idea is to establish any possible bond between juror and attorney.

What about intelligence? The consultants have an answer to that, too. As Gonda noted: "Jurors with high intelligence tend to be more influenced than jurors of low intellectual ability by persuasive . . . logical arguments. Conversely, jurors with high intelligence are less susceptible than jurors with lower intelligence to . . . unsupported generalities or false, illogical, irrelevant arguments. . . ."[14]

The implication is clear. "A highly emotional argument could totally backfire if presented to a jury composed of engineers and accountants, an intelligent group more likely to be swayed by hard facts."[15] The other side of the coin, clearly, is to avoid highly technical testimony before a less educated jury, "since an uneducated group would be more receptive to an emotionally charged appeal."[16]

Some critics might say that this is advice to pander to the jury—but haven't lawyers always pandered in order to win their cases? Others might say that the wise old country lawyer either knew or intuitively came up with exactly the same techniques. And one might note also that in legal training—both on and off the job—such matters of tactics and preparation are duly addressed. A more disturbing criticism though, is the cost—national consultants or even home-based social scientists don't come cheap. In 1981, the *Wall Street Journal* noted that fees, depending on the case and the work performed, can run from $20,000 to $250,000. Neither the proverbial "little man" nor the "little" lawyer may be able to afford such luxury in preparing and conducting a case. "This is great for rich people with unlimited budgets," says attorney Bleecher of Los Angeles, but "if you used these people in a garden-variety case, you'd soon go broke."[17]

New York attorney Boise, veteran of the IBM case against California Computer, also warns attorneys against too great a dependence on the behavioral consultants. "Persuading the jury is important, and they help here," he says. "But you're also trying to convince the trial judge, and he will give instructions to the jury."[18]

For that matter, judges have also been the subject of psychological or behavioral study in recent years. The aforementioned book, *The Psychology of the Courtroom,* includes studies suggesting that judges, too, are often swayed by factors other than the law or the facts before them. Their own group affiliations bear upon their selection as judges in the first place, and their religious, ethnic, and political background also matters after they're on the bench. Political background appears to be especially influential—would any Republican be surprised by findings reported in *The Psychology of the Courtroom* that Democratic judges tend to be more "liberal" in the courtroom than Republican judges?

Whether consciously or subconsciously, other factors influence judges, too. Variables such as organizational affiliation, class background, religion, and even tenure on the bench have been correlated with liberal or conservative decision making. In a study of federal judges in draft evasion cases, judges who had draft-age sons tended to be more severe in sentencing draft evaders than other judges were. Another study found that federal district judges in the South who voted in race relations cases after the 1954 Supreme Court decision on school desegregation were most likely to be *pro*-integration when they also were Republican in their politics, were more cosmopolitan, and had less (if any) experience in holding state political office. Obviously, such biases can influence other types of cases as well—civil and criminal.

Basically, the essays collected in *The Psychology of the Courtroom* confirm what many lawyers have known by intuition and by their own experience in courtroom situations. The more scientific picture that emerges, though, is somewhat discouraging confirmation of age-old lore. Litigation is often influenced, even controlled, by factors unrelated to the ideal of rational or fair outcome in the trial process—that is, by irrelevancies such as which party speaks first and which speaks last or by characteristics of a party to the case that have nothing to do with guilt or liability but rather concern gender, race, socioeconomic status, or even attractiveness. Furthermore, it is difficult to ferret out and exclude jurors with built-in biases, and eyewitnesses testimony is influenced by human frailty and is measured subjectively by jurors applying eccentric yardsticks to credibility. Even the organization and deliberation of juries are influenced by irrational factors. Selection of the foreman apparently is influenced by gender, occupational status, prior experience as a juror, and even position at the jury table. Those who talk the most during jury deliberations, and therefore may have a greater influence on the verdict, tend to be male, well-educated, high in occupational status—and sitting at one end of the jury table or the other.

For students of legal lore—and for veteran lawyers—there is something strikingly familiar in all the "scientific" definition of jury attitudes and concomitant strategy decisions. Philip Corboy of Chicago is one of the most successful personal injury lawyers in the country, and an important part of his success stems from his ability to pick a friendly jury. For Corboy, it is axiomatic to reject retirees, because they live on fixed incomes and thus "are too tight with a buck." Jews and blacks, on the other hand, are prime candidates, because "they have tasted discrimination and therefore tend to identify with the underdog plaintiff." He likes blue-collar workers as well: "They empathize more with victims because their own bodies are their livelihood."[19]

It is not surprising, however, that the ideal juror on the defense side is often the opposite of Corboy's ideal. According to Max Wildman, a leading defense lawyer in Chicago, speaking of how he selects jurors: "You have to find people able to resist the natural impulse to give the plaintiff the moon, and that's not easy." Wildman welcomes retired people living on fixed incomes and older blue-collar and middle management workers: "They are accustomed to shifting for themselves and are usually conservative with awards." On the other hand, Wildman shuns younger jurors because of what he terms their "tendency to have a social-worker, do-gooder mentality." Yet in his jury selection, Wildman will often strive for a racial and class variety in order to create dissension. "A disunified jury," he says, "rarely grants large awards."[20]

Judges, too, are subject to the "corruption" of such irrational influences as their group affiliations and general attitudes. The "science" of courtroom drama—which is painful, real-life drama—seems to cry out for a more rational approach to deciding who gets what after injury. The picture that emerges from scholarly writing and from trials of actual cases corroborates the thesis that the outcomes of lawsuits are determined by various irrational factors as well as by reason and fairness. We are struck again and again by the "accidents" of litigation in accident litigation.

But what is the alternative to the courtroom? All the vicissitudes of a trial are hard to dispense with in criminal cases—and in many civil cases as well. We can hardly punish people criminally without exhaustive exhumation and examination of the applicable facts and law; and a similar situation arises when the question is whether to burden a party for breach of contract that threatens insolvency for one party or the other. The adversary system seems as good as, if not better than, any other means of resolving the merits of such cases. But in regard to accidents involving personal injuries, it seems worthwhile to explore alternatives in the form of insurance arrangements that can dispense with the need for most litigation.[21] The more we know about (mis)judgments in such cases, the more we are pointed to the wisdom of insurance-based alternatives to litigation.

4

Expert Confusion

IN the late 1970s, Robert J. diGrazia was a police chief. He had been in charge of the police departments of Boston and St. Louis County and then found his way to the helm of the police force in suburban Montgomery County, Maryland, on the outskirts of Washington, D.C. In 1977, his last year there, his annual salary was $52,811.

Six years later, diGrazia was making as much or more as a litigation consultant and expert witness on police matters—a new career he had not really planned: "How did I get into consulting work? I got fired."[1] At first, diGrazia had hoped to find a new police chief post somewhere, but then a lawyer called seeking his help in a civil court case. Then another lawyer called—and diGrazia began advertising his availability and expertise. By 1983, things were going so well that he was earning more than his salary had been in affluent Montgomery County. His expert testimony was sometimes "against" police parties, sometimes "for" them; it ran from personal injury cases involving hot pursuit to improper use of firearms.

In the larger view, diGrazia represents another relatively new trend in American litigation. The same scientific approach that studies jury psychology has also produced the widespread "expert-witness" phenomenon. And it is another high-cost item; many people today who are experts in their various fields derive a handsome living from multitudinous appearances in trials across the land. In a 1983 study of the expert-witness trend, the *Washington Post* noted: "Whatever the court, the case, or the complexity of the dispute, it's a new axiom of law that you can't have enough experts. In an age of litigation, expert witnesses have become an expensive but increasingly common addition to the legal process—and a trend that judges and jurors, lawyers and even the experts themselves view with some reservation."[2]

The so-called professional witnesses even advertise in legal journals. One recurring ad in a trial lawyers' monthly magazine shows a doctor in a white coat—in a boxing stance, complete with boxing gloves—urging that he be hired to help prepare medical malpractice cases. According to the *Post*, experts offer their expertise "on seemingly arcane subjects such as nighttime bicycle accidents, electric explosions, lawn-mower injuries and forklift accidents, and lawyers are snapping up their services."[3]

In 1982, the *New York Times* likewise noted that "experts show up in courtrooms these days to testify on just about everything."[4] The focus of the *Times* piece, as the "latest vogue," was forensic psychologists—"a variety of experts that some lawyers claim are nothing more than specialists in common sense." Traditionally, the testimony of psychologists has had widely accepted bearing on such matters as sanity, child custody, and the like. Generally, psychologists have tended not to supplant, but to supplement, the appearance of psychiatrists—giving testimony, for instance, on clinical testing. Now, however, they are taking a role in product liability cases. As the *Times* noted: "More and more lawyers are asking psychologists to develop tests that will convince a jury that there is a solid scientific answer to such questions as whether a warning label was written so that the average consumer would heed it or whether a product's design made it inherently unsafe."[5]

The same article linked the new trend to the establishment of joint degree programs in law and psychology at the University of Nebraska, Arizona, and Maryland (in league with nearby Johns Hopkins) and at Villanova (together with Hahnemann Medical School). But there are doubters about such scientific bases for the increasing use of expert witnesses. According to Irving Younger, once a judge himself and more recently a trial attorney in Washington, D.C.: "Juries tend to be impressed with anything that sounds like science. If you introduce scientific jargon and scientific measurements, they are more apt to accept what they are told than to use their own common sense, which is what jurors are supposed to bring to the case."[6] Michael F. Colley, a leading plaintiffs' lawyer, admits that "juries vote based on their impressions, their feelings, their biases, and their prejudices, not the facts of the case." Thus, he states, the credibility of expert witnesses, who are supposedly testifying on matters of scientific precision, often turns on "their language, style, and body codes and cues."[7]

As one might expect, the founder of the University of Nebraska's joint degree program in law and psychology justifies the use of experts. Bruce Sales, a lawyer-psychologist who more recently was director of the University of Arizona's joint law and psychology program, says:

The justice system is based on all kinds of assumptions about human behavior. The law relating to jury instructions assumes that jurors will understand what the judge says. The law relating to eyewitness identification assumes that people who see someone for a very brief time in a high-stress situation will remember and accurately identify what they saw. A lot of the assumptions can be shown to be untrue.[8]

The numerous and various experts available for court testimony are legion in their number and variety, one-sided, "two-sided," indispensable or a curse on the legal fraternity, depending on one's point of view—especially regarding cost. "I've paid experts as much as $5,000 a day," reports Harvey Weitz of Manhattan, a former president of the New York State Trial Lawyers Association. "Without them, I have no case, and they know it. Almost anything today calls for the expert witness."[9]

Pity, then, the "little" plaintiff or defendant in the "little" case. In a study sponsored by the National Center for State Courts, the researchers found one court insisting that plaintiffs in the most routine personal injury case must produce a doctor and an economist or face dismissal of their suit. The study noted: "Yet the cost of retaining the two, coupled with the attorney's fee, made it financially unrewarding to take claims of less than $10,000 to trial, even if victory appeared assured." Thus, people with legitimate grievances were denied their day in court and were forced to settle for relatively little, or nothing, for their pains.

"Many people simply can't afford an expert," acknowledges one member of the bench, Federal District Judge Joyce Hens Green of Washington, D.C. She says that there's no question the cost factor is "a barrier to entry for people of limited means."[10] Another drawback to the experts trend of recent years is the disturbing probability that any resourceful attorney can find an expert or two to support his client's case. "Some experts are one-sided," says Dr. Lawrence I. Kaplan, a psychiatrist and neurologist in New York who earns $200,000 a year as a legal consultant and expert witness. Kaplan says he is not one-sided, because "I see patients for both plaintiff and defense lawyers."[11] He evaluates their disabilities from his two expert points of view, then reports back to his lawyer-client. "If his report favors the case," says the *New York Times Magazine*, "Dr. Kaplan may be called to testify. If it's unfavorable, the lawyer gets another expert."[12]

Judge Patrick E. Higginbotham of the U.S. Fifth Circuit Court of Appeals in Dallas, however, hints that even the experts are subject to the vicissitudes of courtroom psychology: "Our adversary system gets another participant, another champion. Sometimes that's done by experts almost without apology, but far more often it comes from a human tendency to identify with the side that you're testifying for. Even the most conscientious expert can get caught up in it: When the other side challenges you on the stand, the natural tendency is to respond in kind." The federal jurist adds: "People who don't view themselves as advocates become just that, and the danger is that an inexperienced jury may not be able to detect this partisan cast. A jury might be bamboozled."[13]

Should it be any surprise that the expert's own lawyer may put on the pressure? Massachusetts Superior Court Judge Robert J. Hallisey calls it "a seduction process": "They try to get them to go as far as they can in their direction. You have some experts who are trying to play it straight, and others who are prostitutes, but the guy who is trying to play it straight is at a disadvantage. He hedges and qualifies things on cross-examination, and as a result doesn't seem as convincing as the charming faker who might be testifying for the other side."[14]

Even a veteran expert witness agrees that there are pitfalls. Ralph L. Barnett, an engineering professor at the Illinois Institute of Technology, said in a speech to the American Society of Mechanical Engineers in 1977: "If you're really trying to tell the truth, the whole truth and nothing but the truth, you will find that the courtroom is just about the hardest place in the world to comply with these three things which you have sworn to do before you start your testimony."[15]

Attorney Younger, not only a former judge but also a former law school professor and an authority on the rules of evidence, claims that many of the issues submitted to the experts are only matters of opinion anyway: "We pretend those are factual questions and call economists to testify, but they're simply a matter of opinion. And in virtually every case in this country in which experts end up on the witness stand, there are vast possibilities for honest differences of opinion."[16]

Younger notes that in cases where opinion can reasonably differ, "each lawyer simply scouts around until he finds an expert who has an opinion that comports with his client's interest." But, he also says, "Experts can testify in good faith and still be testifying to opposites."[17] A classic example was the criminal trial of John W. Hinckley, Jr., the disturbed young man who attempted to assassinate President Reagan in 1981. The opposing teams attempted to show that, at the time, Hinckley was insane (defense view) or *not* insane (prosecution view). The total estimated cost of experts hired by the two sides was $350,000 to $450,000.

Such "experting" apparently had its start in fourteenth-century England, where the courts themselves produced the experts, initially from such fields as shipping or accounting. The adversary system, developed later in the United States, slowly moved away from the court's experts to those produced by the adversaries—but not without an occasional word of caution, such as the warning by the New York Court of Appeals in 1884 that the views of the experts "cannnot fail to be warped by a desire to promote the cause in which they are enlisted." It would be better, said the same court, to rely upon the "impartial, unbiased judgments of 12 jurors of common sense and common experience."[18]

That is not the view held in many quarters in today's technological age, though. According to Judge Higginbotham of the Fifth Appellate Court: "Experts are very, very important. They teach you. They can explain things to a jury that no ordinary citizen is experienced in. Someone has got to be able to translate a complicated, scientific subject into terms that laymen can understand."[19]

At their best, the experts avoid the common courtroom frailties of skewed perception, faulty memory, bias, or personal interest, say Richard Van Duizend and Michael J. Saks, who conducted a study on scientific evidence in litigation for the National Center for State Courts. As also noted by Saks, an associate professor of social psychology at Boston College, the defense in many criminal cases fails, often for lack of resources, to rebut apparently expert testimony presented by the prosecution. Yet the prosecution evidence is often weak, he adds. As evidence, he cites a nationwide study discovering that 71 percent of police crime labs were wrong, within a sample time frame, in their blood tests, 51 percent in their identifications of paint samples, and 28 percent in their identifications of firearms. Saks says: "The defense ought to be finding these errors. But the defense frequently doesn't do that. It may be that the aura of science intimidates criminal defense attorneys. It may also be that they assume the prosecution's experts are competent." As he goes on to note, however: "The defense also has to have time and money if it is to challenge the prosecution experts. In a multi-million-dollar civil case, money to pay experts is no problem...."[20]

For some, of course, it is a problem. But the experts trend has become ubiquitous in the big-money civil cases. According to legal writer John A. Jenkins in the *New York Times Magazine* of December 11, 1983: "As lawsuits have proliferated, so has the number of experts whose testimony can make or break a case in court. . . . They represent a major part of the American litigation industry."[21]

William Mazer of Glen Echo, Maryland, who makes $100 an hour as an expert on electrical accidents, also wrote *The Electric Accident Investigation Handbook*, published in 1982. His expertise is valuable in cases involving electric shock and the arc explosions that erupt when high-voltage electricity heats the air. He finds it fascinating detective work to assemble the accident picture from pieces of wreckage, witness accounts, and even the sound, color, timing, and odor of the explosion in question. With a national average of 10,000 serious injuries resulting from electrical accidents every year, he says that "there's no shortage" in the demand for his specialized services.[22]

A perhaps more predictable line of work is that of Francis M. McDermott of McLean, Virginia, who left a perfectly good job at the Federal Aviation Administration in 1960 to become a legal expert in analyzing data from the cockpits of crashed airplanes. Over the next twenty-three years, he "worked" more than 1,600 crash cases and developed subspecialties such as analyzing voice prints and enhancing tape recordings. Among his clients was Korean Air Lines, which asked him to study air-controller data stemming from the downing of the airline's Flight 007 over Russian territory in 1983.

"Years ago," says McDermott, "if you lost a light airplane, you were talking of between $2,000 and $4,000, and an insurance company would write a check and say, 'Go buy a new one.'" No longer, of course; now the loss sums are gigantic, the injury suits are legion, and the experts are essential to explain, or claim, who was at fault. "I just happened to be in there when it was breaking," adds McDermott, whose fee is $80 an hour.[23]

Forgery is the specialty of David Crown of Fairfax, Virginia, another government worker whose background made him an expert. First a postal inspector, Crown subsequently headed the CIA's questioned-documents laboratory for fifteen years. He then went into business for himself in 1982 as an expert in separating the phony document from the real—a major asset in legal cases dealing with wills, medical records, insurance papers, and the like. "It's like doing puzzles," says Crown, who spends forty hours a week in a home laboratory equipped for analyses of inks, paper and handwriting samples. "When I come up with the right answer, I know I have the right answer. I get excited by my work." The excitement evidently carries over into the adversary arena of the courtroom. "It's a challenge. The [opposing] lawyer asks the questions—but I know more about documents than he does, so it's kind of an even match."[24] This seems to suggest that even with his "right answer," it's a 50-50 proposition as to whether a jury will believe him.

Although many legal cases now rely heavily on all kinds of expert testimony, medical malpractice suits—by tradition and, indeed, by definition (in that a court won't hear a patient's case without an expert to support it)—are built from the ground up on testimony by expert witnesses. By definition, too, this means medical expert against medical expert; the credentials on each side are usually impressive, yet the judgments thrown before the laymen jury are entirely contradictory. (One gets the impression in a case involving an amputation, the defense expert will testify that the limb will probably grow right back, with the plaintiff's expert equally confident the amputation will spread—with the hapless jury left to decide which to believe.) Here, too, professional must critique professional—a delicate situation. According to legal writer John Jenkins, the American Medical Association has frowned upon the activity of doctors "who make it part of their occupation" to testify frequently as experts but considers it ethical for AMA members to testify as experts aloof from partisanship in the courtroom. Nonetheless, many doctors find the practice disquieting. "I find it very disheartening," says Dr. Raymond Scalettar, chairman of the AMA's Committee on Professional Liability in 1983 and a former president of the Medical Society of the District of Columbia. "I have no way of quantifying this, but I know there's a cadre of physicians who are supplementing their income by testifying against other physicians." Notes Scalettar, too: "It's a lucrative endeavor."[25]

If some doctors are seen as overzealous in their willingness to "correct" the profession, there have also been efforts to discourage critical testimony. In a 1977 episode, an orthopedic surgeon from Florida and a neurosurgeon from New Jersey appeared in Maryland to testify in a malpractice suit against Dr. Edmond J. McDonnell, medical director of Children's Hospital in Baltimore and an eminent surgeon. The *Washington Post* reported:

> At McDonnell's request, the two witnesses were contacted by medical professors they had studied under and warned that transcripts of their testimony would be sent to their respective medical societies. Both said they felt intimidated; one said he feared he would be treated as a "violator of the code of silence" and would be unable to get medical-board certification.[26]

McDonnell later was reprimanded by the state medical discipline commission, an action affirmed by the Maryland Court of Special Appeals, which called his action "outrageous," "clearly morally wrong," and tantamount to "an endeavor to obstruct justice."

More typical, and indicative of how the expert-witness syndrome usually works, is a power-tool case Philip Corboy handled in Chicago. As part of the $20,000 the personal injury lawyer spent in preparing for trial, he immersed himself in the abstruse technicalities of metallurgy, for his blinded client's suit would have to claim a defect in the tool had let loose a tiny chip of steel. After examining more than twenty books on metallurgy and allied subject matter, Corboy even had the tool sent to California for close inspection by an electron microscope large enough to encompass the entire tool in one view. He took about twenty depositions from various experts and witnesses and had 100 exhibits prepared, among them poster-size blowups of the chip and the tool. The final step, though, which was essential to winning his case, was his choice of expert witnesses to appear in court. One was an industrial metallurgist from Chicago; the second was a professor of metallurgy from Long Beach State College in California. According to the metallurgist, it was a failure in uniformity in the chemical composition of the tool, among other defects, that caused the chipping. Not to be outdone, the defense produced a professor from the Illinois Institute of Technology in Chicago, who likewise "proved" in exhaustive detail that there was nothing wrong with the metal of the tool.

Corboy, however, is also an attorney who believes that a lawyer's worst sin "is to bore the jury." In his view, "It isn't enough to get jurors who will find the defendant liable; they must also be willing to give the plaintiff big money." In the power-tool case, before finally presenting his client in the company of a seeing-eye dog, Corboy made elaborate use of color photos of the injuries to his client's one "good" eye (his other eye having been previously blinded). Then, in his closing argument, by Corboy's own description, he "pulled out all the stops." He spent an hour regaling the jury with the sheer hell of a blind person's life and ended with an emotional plea for justice that would offset his client's sentence to "a life of perpetual midnight."[27] Corboy won his case—to the tune of a $752,500 settlement while the jury was out.

In another personal liability case, the issue seemed to be simply how or why a suburban Maryland man was hurt when he fell off a ladder. Taking the case to court, he said that it was the ladder's fault; it was defective. The manufacturer, however, said that it was the user's fault; he had placed the ladder's feet on uneven ground. Enter, at this point, the experts.

For the injured plaintiff came an engineering expert who said that the aluminum ladder was at fault because of the way it was extruded—or formed when pumped, in more or less heated liquid state, from a container of aluminum. According to this expert, problems with the extrusion or tempering process—rather than the actual ladder design—made the upper "fly" section defective.

The manufacturer then produced an expert who contended that the extrusion process guaranteed uniform results. This "accident reconstruction expert" displayed a complete scale model of the plaintiff's house and the ladder, then testified that the plaintiff "probably set his ladder in place improperly and then landed on top of it when it fell."[28]

Now came the plaintiff with doctor-witnesses who said that his fall could have caused a brief drop in his blood pressure and arterial collapse and that even if it lasted only minutes, such collapse could have made him impotent. But doctors produced by the defense testified that any such arterial damage might well have been caused by his being a smoker and a drinker.

In such a situation, with the experts at odds, what is a jury to think? By the time this case went to the jury, after a week of testimony, "Nobody was arguing anything else beyond the experts," recalled the jury foreman, Terry N. Chamberlain.[29] The jury continued that argument for eight hours, at which time the judge declared a mistrial and sent everybody home. Eventually, an out-of-court settlement was reached. Melvin Bergman, the Maryland man's attorney, says that he has only one regret about the case—that he did not call even another expert, a metallurgist.

In another Washington-area case, attorney Thomas E. Silfen of suburban Montgomery County, Maryland, served on a jury considering the allegedly extensive emotional injury to a young woman subjected to a relatively slight personal injury.

The sequence of events at the trial was familiar to Silfen, an active trial lawyer: "First came the fact witnesses, principally the accident victim and her husband, to tell their stories and to grab the jury's sympathy. Together they related the unhappy effects of accident-related stress on their work, their marital relations and their lives in general."

Next came "a parade of experts"—a doctor, a psychologist, a psychiatrist, and a psychiatrist-neurologist—"each trying to demonstrate . . . how his science supported one or the other of two directly conflicting views: i.e., how the alleged stress was (or was not) related to the accident and how it was (or was not) properly treated by psychotherapy."[30]

After a day and a half of testimony—the facts taking two to three hours and the experts consuming a full day—the jury retired to consider the case. Juror Silfen had filled two pads with notes and yet still felt "woefully underinformed."[31] Left to his own devices, he would have reserved judgment for a time, reviewed the facts, tried to understand the medical "lore," and looked at the applicable law. But the jury was back in the courtroom in less than two hours with a money award for the plaintiff.

How could the jurors possibly have sifted through all the contradictory medical evidence so fast? "For starters," states Silfen, "we largely ignored the experts."[32] In effect, they had canceled each other out.

"I became part of a common-sense consensus," he wrote in an interesting comment on how juries may in fact *work*. He equated that consensus with "a collective lunge for equity that was not based at all on the lawyerly analysis that law school and 15 years of practice otherwise make mandatory. Together the jury exercised what might be described as mass intuition: a . . . gut reaction."[33]

And what about all that testimony by the experts? According to Silfen:

> They were reasonably good witnesses and apparently eminent men in their fields, but as always in litigation, their opinions were directly in conflict. (For example, the plaintiff's experts said that the emotional injury was real, flowed from the accident and required psychiatric treatment, and the defendant's expert asserted just the opposite.) There was no rational way that the jury could decide, on the medical merits, who was right—whether, as Dr. X maintained, plaintiff's only real need was "to get back on the horse," or whether Dr. Y was correct that elaborate (and expensive) "desensitization training" was appropriate.[34]

You have to wonder, if you or a loved one were critically injured and permanently disabled, whether you'd want your financial future to turn on a battle of warring experts—with a thoroughly confused jury caught in between.

5

The Litigation Lottery

ALTHOUGH Americans, as a group, live longer than ever, accident and illness still descend unexpectedly to impair that lengthened life. Indeed, by the year 2000, according to experts at the Menninger Foundation, *half* of America's population will be physically disabled, chronically ill, or older than 65. Millions of the disabled are already among us—struck down, it once was thought, by blind chance. And who is to blame? Sometimes, it appears, no one.

William Raspberry, a perceptive columnist appearing in the *Washington Post*, tells the tale of Dennis Butler. As a young boy and then as a college student, Butler spent much of his time as a volunteer in a neighborhood therapeutic recreation center near his home in Washington, D.C., helping the handicapped people there. As a youngster, he performed small chores: "I was too small to lift them or anything." Later, he helped out as a chaperone on camping trips or with the Special Olympics for the physically disabled. Sometimes he simply helped the center's patrons take a shower.

The Washington youth eventually went away to prestigious Williams College in New England to major in German. He was also an active skier, rock climber, spelunker, and white-water rafter.

While skiing at Williams on ski patrol in January 1984, Dennis "took an edge"—which means that he hit a patch of ice and fell. In seconds, he had suffered permanent spinal cord damage. And now *he* is handicapped.

As his father, Charles Butler, said later: "One minute you're a happy, healthy person, skiing downhill. The next minute you can't even scratch your nose."[1]

Another scenario played out in the Washington area in the mid-1980s and described in the *Washington Post* was even more appalling than Dennis Butler's unhappy fate. In October 1982, young Cory Watts rode his motorcycle into the concrete median of heavily traveled Shirley Highway in the Arlington, Virginia, segment of Interstate 95. Then 19 and a recent high school graduate, Cory was wearing a protective helmet, as required by law, but in the crash the helmet cracked above the nape of his neck. He was severely injured—so severely that he was in a coma for three months after his accident.

Left with brain damage and partial paralysis thereafter, Cory was mildly retarded intellectually and functioned on the level of a 12-year-old child, according to later trial testimony. In 1985, he still required constant care at home and continuing medical attention; family members testified that he was forgetful and that they had to cut his food into pieces so that he could feed himself. Unhappily, too, three years after the accident the medical bills were still mounting, at the rate of $50,000 a year; they came to $500,000 in all.

The youth's accident was not the family's first bout with adversity. Cory's father, Roy, survived his experience as an American fighter pilot in the Korean War only to contract polio in the late 1950s. As a result, Roy Watts, a contracting officer for the Navy, was partially crippled and could walk only with the aid of a cane or crutches. According to family friends, his wife, Cordelia, took his mishap in stride. Her son's misfortune years later apparently took a greater toll on her inner strength.

"You don't see many people like Cordelia," said a guidance counselor from Cory's high school in Alexandria, Virginia. "She had so many disappointments, and she just shrugged them off. Roy had polio and that was hard on her. But Cory was her pride and joy and it just killed her to see him torn apart like that."[2]

And Patricia Tiernan, a rehabilitation therapist who worked with the injured youth for two years, noted: "She fought for that kid from the moment he had the accident. She was angry and she was tough. She just loved that boy so much you could see the pain inside her."[3]

The Watts family sued Bell Helmets of Norwalk, California, the makers of Cory's safety helmet, for $10 million. Their contention was that the helmet was defective in design. The federal court jury considering the suit deliberated for eight hours, then decided against Cory. "I didn't feel good about that verdict, I don't think anybody did," said one of the jurors later. "Everybody would have loved to give them the money. They obviously needed it. But the evidence was so strongly in favor of Bell. We had no choice."[4]

Coming at the end of a three-day trial in U.S. District Court in Alexandria, the verdict was delivered on Wednesday, July 10, 1985. Two hours later, Cordelia Watts, 52, persuaded her husband Roy, 61, to leave their Alexandria home on a cooked-up errand, then shot her son Cory and herself to death in the backyard. "That boy was just falling apart mentally and physically," said a shocked neighbor who knew the family well. "And it was killing his parents, too. I guess when she lost this suit she just gave up."[5]

Left behind were more than $30,000 in legal debts, according to economist Richard Lurito, who had appeared in the trial as an expert witness on behalf of the family. "They are dead broke," said Lurito. "They invested everything they had in this case and it wiped them out. There is absolutely nothing left."[6]

Fred C. Alexander, Jr., defense counsel for Bell in the product liability suit, was also shaken. "What can you say about something like that?" he asked. "Nobody could possibly anticipate it. We are all horrified. The people at Bell can only send the deepest condolences."[7]

Others said that Roy and Cordelia Watts quite naturally feared that someday soon there simply wouldn't be enough money to provide Cory's basic medical care. Rehabilitation therapist Tiernan, who lost a child of her own to an auto accident, noted that the average $18,000 *monthly* cost of therapy for a bed-ridden patient is so calamitous that many families despair. "The scope of this tragedy is huge," she said. "There is nothing more horrible in the world than to wonder what is going to happen to someone you love if they are incapacitated. It would make anyone sick."[8]

Not all liability law suits end so tragically, of course. In many cases, the aggrieved plaintiffs win ample sounding, often astounding, awards. Even in the event of successful litigation, though, the repercussions can be bittersweet at best. Obviously, the injured party remains injured. Furthermore, . . . well, let's take a look at a medical malpractice case that arose in New York City, as reported by the *New York Times* in 1985.

The story begins with a pregnancy—the first for Marjorie Grossman, a math teacher and married for nearly eight years to David Grossman, a part-time instructor at City University. Mrs. Grossman, 30, became pregnant toward the end of 1980.

To all appearances, her condition advanced normally for the next nine months. As her expected delivery date of August 6 approached, her obstetrician, Dr. Milton Falik, was preparing to go on vacation. The *Times* noted, incidentally, that as of 1980, obstetricians in Queens, where the Grossman case took place, paid $45,196 a year for $1 million in malpractice liability insurance. (As we shall see, rates have skyrocketed since 1980 in New York and elsewhere.)

Since Dr. Falik would be away, he introduced Mrs. Grossman to an associate who would be "covering for him," Dr. Fritz A. Van Gessel. Dr. Van Gessel would be the physician who would actually deliver her baby at Hillcrest General Hospital in Queens.

The expected delivery date, August 6, passed by uneventfully—no baby. But that was not unusual for a first pregnancy. As the *Times* also noted, meanwhile: "Mr. and Mrs. Grossman led a simple if not always easy life. Married eight years, together they earned less than $30,000 a year and were seriously in debt."[9]

After some days in suspense, Mrs. Grossman became concerned by the delay. According to the *Times*, "Dr. Van Gessel arranged for her to be seen by another doctor, had tests ordered and told her everything was fine."[10]

On Friday, August 21, the day after the tests, the expectant mother awoke in "excruciating" pain. She and her husband raced to Hillcrest. There, a first-year resident doctor examined her and connected her to a fetal monitor. He then sent her home with the explanation that she was not sufficiently dilated for the birthing process. (In trial later, however, the same first-year resident would testify that he hadn't known how to read the fetal monitor.)

Later the same day, Mrs. Grossman went back to the hospital and finally gave birth to a girl—to be named Alissa. But the infant had "problems," she was told. The "problem" turned out to be cerebral palsy. Alissa could be expected to live into her 70s, but she would remain retarded and paralyzed for life. She would require 24-hour assistance at home, at an estimated $80 a day, plus room and board costs—for a total of $29,000 a year, or more than $2 million over her anticipated lifespan, according to later trial testimony. Her lifetime need for diapers alone would cost $700,000, calculated at $10,000 a year since she would require expensive adult diapers for fifty of the years. Again according to trial testimony, she would lose an estimated $800,000 in projected earning capacity for an individual with a high school education.

What could the young, already financially strapped couple do? Quite apart from the emotional impact on them, how would they meet such a financial burden? Many weeks later, Mrs. Grossman's father suggested a lawsuit. He had been talking with friends, and the friends had suggested consulting with the law firm of Pegalis and Waxman in Great Neck, Long Island, near Queens. The couple paid a visit to Steven Pegalis, who said he would look into the case and, if it had merit, would take it on a contingency fee basis. He then subpoenaed the infant Alissa's medical records.

In a few days, he called the Grossmans on the telephone. "He was ecstatic," said Mrs. Grossman later. "He said, 'It's unbelievable—it's so clear-cut.'"[11]

As the attorney reconstructed the case, the very morning Mrs. Grossman first visited Hillcrest, the instrument measuring her baby's heartbeat indicated signs of distress. "Some irregularity was even apparent," he said, "in the tests reported to Dr. Van Gessel the day before."[12]

Whereas Dr. Van Gessel had told the Grossmans that the infant's problems were caused by the umbilical cord at delivery, Pegalis maintained that the real problem was the extended pregnancy: "The placenta had begun to disintegrate and was not providing enough oxygen."[13] His contention was that the resulting brain damage could have been avoided if Van Gessel and Hillcrest had induced labor or had performed a surgical Caesarean delivery. The Grossmans, with Pegalis as their attorney, sued almost everybody in sight—the vacationing Dr. Falik, Van Gessel, as the doctor who delivered Alissa, the hospital. According to the *Times*, "Mr. Pegalis told the other lawyers in the case that he believed it was good for $3 million. He said jury verdicts for $2.5 million had been upheld in similar cases. Still, lawyers for Dr. Falik and Dr. Van Gessel—each of whom carried $1 million in insurance—refused to settle. A trial was scheduled."[14]

Mrs. Grossman was not entirely comforted. "I was down on the whole thing," she later said of the lawsuit. "It was not going to change things. But Dave was more gung-ho. He said they should pay for what they did."[15]

Since Dr. Falik had apparently done nothing wrong, the case against him was soon dismissed as being without merit. Still, his insurance company had to pay his legal fees to that point. As the trial unfolded, meanwhile, the inexperienced resident who had examined Mrs. Grossman and had sent her home acknowledged his failure to read the infant monitor correctly.

Just before the case went to the jury, the parties agreed to a $2.5 million settlement. Although Dr. Van Gessel had died, his malpractice insurer paid $1 million, the extent of his coverage. Hillcrest hospital provided the extent of its coverage—$1 million—and paid an additional $500,000 on its own.

The settlement may have resolved the issue, but it didn't make the principles in the drama happy. "It was in no way a concession of wrongdoing," said Bruce Brady, an attorney representing Dr. Van Gessel's estate. And Dr. Falik, who left his obstetrics practice in part because of the Grossman case, said: "For 50 years I've been an obstetrician. I reached the stage that I persuaded my son not to be an obstetrician. I wouldn't let a dog pick up obstetrics."[16]

For their part, even after deducting the one-third fee that was due attorney Pegalis (about $830,000), the Grossman couple wound up sudden millionaires. By early 1985, they were driving two cars and were planning a summer vacation in Europe. They had moved from a cramped, rent-stabilized apartment to a four-bedroom house filled with furniture beyond their dreams.

Was this an enviable bonanza for the Grossmans? Not really, even though certain aspects of their life have been made easier. "It can't change anything for Alissa," said Mrs. Grossman. "There is no amount of money that will make this easier. I will never have the joy of running out for the newspaper with my daughter beside me. And I am the one who has to listen to her scream—out of sheer frustration—knowing that this could have been prevented."[17]

Her husband, whose part-time job at City University paid $8,000 annually, said, "We're like lottery winners—except we didn't win the lottery."[18]

In truth, they didn't. Even aside from their child's agony, they still have financial problems. The nearly $1.7 million of Alissa's settlement remaining after the legal fees should earn at least $120,000 a year in interest, which is normally taxable. By court order, however, Alissa's parents may spend just $3,000 a month ($36,000 annually) on her care: "They must return to court for special permission if they need more."[19] According to the *Times*, the money made them uneasy: "They do not know where to begin spending or investing it, and as they look to the future, they have no idea what it will cost to take care of their daughter."[20]

Still, there was one bottom line that many a parent in an analogous situation would pray for. "Say 20 years from now there is brain surgery that can restore function," noted David Grossman. "It [the money] will allow us to go anywhere to get her the best care in the world."[21]

However, as another bottom line, few parents of normal children would trade places with the Grossmans. How many would willingly take on a child who as a baby was in constant discomfort; who required special chairs, swings, toys; who could not turn herself over or hold a bottle; and who at age 3 was unable to speak or to lift her head? "From time to time," said the *Times*, "her muscles become so stiff that they are almost locked in place, and to relieve the tension her parents have to wrap her taut little body around a special plastic ball."[22]

As the *Times* also noted, the Grossman case "is not unlike many other large settlements involving infants" in an era of spiraling malpractice suits and the concomitant spiral in insurance premiums for doctors.[23] All over the country, as we shall see, obstetricians like Dr. Falik are abandoning that particularly vulnerable specialty.

Although that may be a loss to society as a whole, not all physicians are perfect. "Malpractice means bad practice," declared the Grossmans' attorney, Steven Pegalis. "If you go through a stop sign, you are negligent. Similarly, doctors have the duty to administer reasonable standards of care."[24] The rub is that both Pegalis and the apparently embittered Dr. Falik have valid points. Indeed, the fact that a case is settled—especially late in the proceedings, as in the Grossmans' case—is usually a signal that both sides fear losing, which is another way of saying that no one knew which way the jury would jump. Not only is the outcome of a case like that of the Grossmans uncertain, but even a favorable verdict will almost certainly be followed by lengthy and uncertain appeals. As mentioned earlier, a good defense lawyer often has as a secondary goal—and sometimes even as a primary goal, if his case is rather weak—to "get error into the record," so that there will be a basis for further and frustrating appeal even after the plaintiff wins at trial. That the end result of litigation can be ashes for many a severely injured accident victim is only too bitterly shown by the fate of Cory and Cordelia Watts.

The public, however, sometimes gets the impression that almost any oddly, unfairly, grievously (and loudly protesting) injured party somehow wins a "free ride" merely by whispering "lawsuit." One reason for such an impression is the publicity generated by large suits with successful outcomes (but rare is the press coverage of a victim who never sues or who settles for moderate compensation).

A prime example of such cause for public disenchantment with large personal injury payments is the controversy and public comment over a 1983 New York City case in which the city's Transit Authority agreed to pay $650,000 to a young man who had jumped in the path of a subway train in a suicide attempt. Milo Stephens, a mental patient, lost an arm, a leg, and part of his other arm in the incident.

A transit attorney blamed New York's law of "comparative negligence," which allows juries or judges to apportion degrees of negligence between claimant and defendant, for the decision to pay the sizable settlement. The *New York Times* took the subway agency to task editorially, saying that "the transit people jumped at an informal settlement because they feared the impression his [Stephens's] appearance would make on a jury." The *Times* also said: "They thought his lawyer might have been able to prove that the train's motorman had ample time to stop the train. The young man's intention to be run down might have struck a jury as mostly, but even then not entirely, to blame for his injuries."[25]

The *Times* was objecting not to the comparative negligence law, which might have resulted in a jury award even in so bizarre a case, but rather to the Transit Authority's "surrender" and its blaming the law. Opined the *Times:* "Instead of blaming the law, the Transit Authority might better ask whether it settled too dearly. Granted Mr. Stephens's lawyer was seeking millions and subway-hating jurors might have awarded them. But why not let city residents—and fare payers—decide whether the subway system owed anything?"[26]

The *Times* itself was then taken to task by a letter writer who was familiar with the city's courts and who argued that the settlement was in the public's best interest. Richard Godosky, head of the Joint Conference Committee on Court Congestion and Related Problems for New York's First and Second Appellate Division Departments, wrote that it would be "an abdication of responsibility" to say "let the jury decide" in all such liability cases. For one thing, he asserted, the resultant court congestion would "vitiate our entire system of justice."

More to the general point, Godosky argued: "In a community where because of jurors' general dislike of it, the Transit Authority is viewed as an easy target by the plaintiffs' trial bar, reasonable settlements, rather than gambling with a jury determination . . . are generally in the best interests of the public." He contended that a trial in the Stephens case, "for the catastrophic injuries he sustained," could have resulted in a verdict of more than $3 million.[27]

But as we know, by no means all plaintiffs win such huge amounts or even come close to a settlement of any real satisfaction. Sometimes, as we have seen, having already been dealt a devastating blow by the injury itself, they go on to lose their case.

In Gaithersburg, Maryland, in April 1978, a 14-year-old junior high student broke his neck in gym class. In attempting a running forward flip behind his teacher's back, he crashed head first onto a tumbling mat. As a result, recounts the *Washington Post*, Michael Harrison was rendered a totally dependent quadraplegic.

Three years later, Michael and his mother, Carol, were in Montgomery County Circuit court in hopes of recovering $3.5 million in damages from the county school system. "You send your children to school and you expect to get them back," explained Carol Harrison. "I don't think he needs to live like a king," she also said. "I just think he needs enough [compensation] to maintain his dignity."[28]

Michael lost his case on the first round in Montgomery County. The next stop was the Maryland Court of Appeals, where Michael's only hope would be a landmark ruling overturning the state's contributory negligence doctrine (as contrasted with New York's comparative negligence law), which says that no accident victim can recover any damages if he himself contributed to the accident in any way. At the time of trial, twelve states (plus the District of Columbia) still retained that rule; by then, the other thirty-eight had gone to comparative negligence, allowing the parties in an accident to share losses in ratio to their degree of fault.

"Human beings make mistakes, that is a fact of life," contended Jacob A. Stein, one of Michael's two attorneys, "and the 38 states that have adopted comparative negligence are dealing with that fact realistically. The remainder are not."[29] The school board argued, however, that the proper forum for any change in Maryland's "all or nothing" rule would be in the state legislature.

A change, noted the *Washington Post* at the time, "would have dramatic impact on the way juries and judges in the state award money damages in the multimillion dollar business of personal injury lawsuits." The outcome of the appeal "means high stakes for insurance companies, who absorb most of the costs of accidents, as well as for the lawyers who bring those cases to court and those who defend against them."[30]

In the lower-court battle, the stakes were more emotional, the details more personal. There, the plaintiff's complaint was that the school system had not properly supervised Michael or trained him against the dangers of amateur gymnastics, according to the *Post*. School board attorney Paul V. McCormick contended that even if there were any negligence by school personnel, Michael himself contributed to his injury by disobeying safety rules and trying his stunt behind the teacher's back.

Some time after the jury of three men and nine women found for the school board, McCormick said: "It was a courageous thing to stand up and tell a quadraplegic that the people you sued are not responsible for what happened to you."[31] The jury foreman, Charlie Oliver, later said, "We all kind of agreed that he [Michael] helped cause the problem." The evidence convinced Oliver, for one, that the teachers "had not done anything wrong."[32]

Another, unidentified juror later sounded more ambivalent, however: "I would have loved to give him some money. I think the whole thing kind of stunk that you have to go in there and say 'No.'"[33]

According to court testimony and Michael's mother, his 24-hour-a-day care in a nursing home in Illinois cost about $20,000 a year and could amount to $1.6 million for life. His costs at the time were being paid by a private health insurer, but that relative luxury would end when he reached the cap on what the insurer was obliged to pay out. The purpose of the suit was to assure the youth continuous care and a more independent existence. "It costs an awful lot to live being a quad," explained Michael in 1983, "especially trying to live like a normal person would and not in an institution."[34]

Even if Maryland had had a comparative negligence rule in effect, there is no assurance that the extent of Michael's own fault would not have resulted in such a scaling down of any award as to leave him in a desperate financial plight—as often happens even in jurisdictions that follow the more lenient comparative negligence rule.

If Michael was offended and surprised by the lower-court jury's verdict against him, others constantly face that blow, too. Proving another person's conduct or product at fault—or one's own lack of fault—is usually a rackingly uncertain business. Studies indicate that plaintiffs in medical malpractice and product liability trials lose about two-thirds to three-quarters of the time.

For Philip Weeda, like so many injury victims, it was one of those "the-next-minute" things. One minute he was in the back of a friend's car leafing through a newspaper, with his feet propped up on the back of the front seat. The next minute, the car had gone out of control and careened onto one side. Weeda, 19, a sophomore at Catholic University in Washington, D.C., and a former football player and weightlifter, was transformed into a quadriplegic, paralyzed from the neck down.

But was it exactly one of those "next-minute" injury situations? In his lawsuit against the District of Columbia, Weeda claimed that the permanent damage to his spinal cord was the fault of rescue personnel who pulled him from the wrecked auto without first placing splints on his broken neck. Weeda's attorney, Joseph Barse, argued that the rescue people prevented paramedics and medical technicians from treating him. Buttressing this allegation was the newsworthy fact, reported on television two days later, that District paramedics and firefighters were at odds over certain rescue procedures.

The scenario had begun with a typical Friday night outing for three young men who had been friends since the fifth grade. They had all once lived within a few blocks of each other in Northwest Washington, near Chevy Chase Circle. They later attended different high schools and colleges, but they often still got together on weekends.

On the night of Weeda's injury, they first spent time at a bar near Tenley Circle watching a baseball playoff game. They then cruised downtown to another bar for more beers—three guys having a good time. They were on their way home when Weeda's friend, who was the owner and driver of their Subaru, attempted a left turn from Florida Avenue onto Connecticut and lost control. He, like Weeda, also suffered a broken neck, but he recovered. Weeda's other friend was only slightly injured. Weeda suffered about as catastrophic an injury as one can suffer.

As so often happens, the injury had a major impact on his family, too. His brother David, an attorney with the federal Food and Drug Administration, left his job and went into private practice to help pay the fast-mounting medical expenses. Philip spent more than three months at Georgetown University Hospital and then nearly a year at the Rusk Institute in New York for rehabilitation therapy. When he returned home, his widowed mother, Helen, was forced to move from their two-story colonial home on Nebraska Avenue to a ranch house in suburban Maryland—it would have cost $40,000 to refit the old house to accommodate her son's handicapped status. The family also had to buy a van for Philip's transportation.

His hospital bills mounted to nearly $350,000 in three years, most of which was paid by his medical insurance. But Philip required frequent hospitalization for complications stemming from his paralysis, such as phlebitis, blood embolisms, urinary problems, and muscle spasms. He had no control over his bodily functions, and he required a daily attendant.

Once he was well enough, he continued to study accounting at Catholic University; only so long as he remained a student would Maryland state vocational rehabilitation funds pay the estimated $13,000 annual cost of the full-time attendant. Philip moved about in an electric wheelchair by activating a lever, since he did have partial use of a bicep in his right arm.

Philip's $4 million lawsuit was originally filed by his brother David, who later said that his suspicions were aroused two days after the accident by the televised news report on the dispute between firefighters and paramedics over rescue procedures. In the trial that followed, the District's attorneys took note of the drinking aspect of the accident. They said that Weeda's own poor judgment, that led to his riding with his drinking friend, contributed to the accident injury.

Unfortunately for Weeda, the case was clouded regarding the applicable precedent in the District's courts for a liability claim against city rescue workers when the claim stemmed from an accident in which both driver and victim admitted to being drunk. On the precedent point, Superior Court Judge Joseph M. Hannon ruled that "although Weeda was negligent, the jury could not consider that in its deliberations" as to the liability for the rescue workers.[35]

Weeda's side had already settled with the driver-friend's insurance company for $50,000, but in January 1983, the Superior Court jury hearing Weeda's claim against city rescue personnel decided against him. "They took the pot of gold away from the end of the rainbow," the paralyzed young man said later. "There's no way we thought we were going to lose."[36]

During the trial, a psychiatrist had testified that Weeda contemplated suicide every day, that he had imagined himself steering his electric wheelchair to the top of his basement stairs and plunging down. After the trial, still claiming that his rescue was mishandled, Philip Weeda said: "I feel outraged. I could be walking. I could have a normal life. I could have had that chance."[37]

His brother David said: "What happened to Philip happened not only to him but to the whole family. It's absolutely devastating."[38] What happened to their mother, said Philip, was also a tragedy. "Every time she sees me in this chair, it hurts her. I think if she could, she would sell her soul to the devil to get me out of it." As for him: "My life is ruined. I'm not a human being any more. Who's going to want me?"[39]

As the cries of the afflicted remind us, there is little the courts can do to restore them physically. It hardly can be denied, however, that money can make a big difference for them and for their families, not only in the quality of care it buys but also in the lessening of anxiety—even desperation—over financial difficulties. It is interesting, though, that studies have shown that injured persons awaiting settlements or verdicts in a liability case seldom get better until the case is resolved. Rehabilitation therapists freely acknowledge their reluctance to accept for treatment those who are in the process of litigation. Given the horrendous delays—not only many months, but many years in the typical serious case—this is a devastating indictment of the law's treatment of even the injured who are eventually paid. In short, recovery in the legal sense impedes recovery in the medical sense.

The point here is that the tort liability system has an insidious way of protecting all parties involved except those with the greatest need of all—the seriously injured people whose losses soon outstrip their financial resources, collateral or otherwise.

Insurance companies are protected by distributing their risks among policyholders with actuarial precision and by reinsuring to the extent that they fear catastrophic losses beyond their own resources. Those who are insured, of course, are protected by that very liability insurance. (As a practical matter, few tort claims are brought against uninsured defendants.) Defense lawyers in liability cases are protected by their guaranteed payment for services rendered, win or lose. Even plaintiffs' attorneys are protected, despite their apparent gamble with contingency fees as a livelihood. The fact is that they can, and often do, turn down cases in which recovery appears unlikely. Furthermore, the typical trial attorney insulates himself from an occasional loss by his "portfolio diversification" of multiple cases in his pipeline. He spreads out his investment of time and effort to avoid serious repercussions from loss of any one case. Injury victims whose economic losses are met by their own collateral sources, such as health insurance, are by definition also relatively well protected. Usually, they are the less seriously injured ones.

Thus, as the field narrows, of all possible parties to tort liability insurance, only the grievously injured party, whose losses are significantly in excess of his collateral sources, is left without a real remedy—except the long, often tortuous, even torturous path of the courts. Even then he waits a seeming eternity to learn when, what, or even *if* he will be paid for his huge—and mounting—losses, as the law proceeds with all deliberate lassitude.

The fact is that those tort liability insurance dollars can be far better used, by devices we will discuss in detail later. Far more than in the processes of the common law, they can provide many seriously injured people with prompt payment of their pressing losses without the agony, uncertainty, and expense of litigation.

6

From Wrecks to Riches

SHORTLY after takeoff from Chicago's O'Hare Airport on May 25, 1979, an American Airlines DC-10 lost its left engine and crashed. The result was the worst disaster in U.S. aviation history to that time, with 275 persons killed. A small army of rescue workers and medical personnel rushed to the scene—and so did a dozen or more of Chicago's notorious ambulance chasers. "Like vultures," said the *Chicago Sun-Times* later, "they pecked at the debris, looking for items that would identify the victims."[1]

The chasers, looking for lawsuit opportunities, had managed to infiltrate police lines at the crash site by posing as emergency personnel. Such behavior is not all that unusual in Chicago. Not only do these vultures chase real accidents, but on the city's Dan Ryan Expressway they have been known to trigger auto accidents deliberately, seriously injuring innocent motorists and their passengers. For a train, bus, or subway accident, dozens of chasers will appear, as if by magic. "They tell the victims, even if they aren't hurt, how to make money by inflating medical bills," adds the *Sun-Times*. "Chasers even 'drop' themselves in these accidents by claiming they were passengers."[2]

In one incident reported by a traffic policeman, a car driven by a known chaser and carrying three passengers suddenly braked hard in front of a second car for no apparent reason. Predictably, the second auto struck the first one in the rear. The traffic officer investigating the case discovered that a taillight fuse was missing from the first vehicle; thus, its warning lights would have been inoperative when the brakes went on. The chaser driving the car was a city employee with a record of felony arrests and convictions, one of them for manslaughter. Apparently, some sort of stage had been set.

Like many American communities, Chicago has its "amateur" chasers—real ambulance drivers, tow-truck operators, cabbies, hospital workers, auto repairmen, and so on. "For $50 or $100, they refer accident victims to lawyers," notes the *Sun-Times*.[3] And there are also the truly dedicated professional chasers, some of them policeofficers. In all, they make up a colorful, even zesty subculture that, in a more harmless, fun-loving world, would lend itself to caricature by a Damon Runyon. In Chicago, however—and in other American cities, too—there is a grim and tawdry aspect to this subculture of not-so-charming thieves. For instance, the *Sun-Times* interviewed two "retired" professionals who had "earned" up to $100,000 a year in "tax-free cash" before quitting their lucrative trade. The money represented referral fees from lawyers who much appreciated the accident tips. In separate interviews, the "retirees" said that 90 percent of their "clients" had been faking their injuries.

It is an unpalatable business in other ways as well. The competition among the city's chasers is so intense that it can lead to shootings and muggings. Both "retirees" had carried handguns while plying their trade. "It's the unwritten code," one of them told the newspaper. "If someone tries to take your money, you blow their head off."[4]

Gangsters and drug dealers are well identified in the public mind with the shoot-'em-down mentality, but who would have thought that one would find the same mentality—at the end of a collusive chain beginning with ambulance chasers—among *lawyers*? The sad commentary on Chicago (luckily, also the home of investigative journalists willing to expose such practices) is that for widespread elements of society, liability law *has* become corrupt. The so-called chasers are only the tip of the iceberg in a racket that also includes both doctors and lawyers. The professional men may not appear in the streets toting handguns, but they are a party to the actions of those who do. According to a well-documented and depressing series of articles on ambulance chasing published by the *Sun-Times* in 1980, many professionals lie, cheat, and steal as common practice.

Nor is the issue simply one of moral outrage. "They really fleece us all," the newspaper notes, "in the form of $3 billion a year in undeserved claims resulting in auto-insurance premiums as much as one-third higher, according to several insurance-fraud experts."[5]

As may be evident, the name of the game is "Auto Accident." In its multifaceted exposé, the *Sun-Times* reported both chasers and law firms that not only allow but urge their clients to inflate or to manufacture medical bills. A further aspect involves medical clinics that accommodate the phony victims with spurious treatment and hospitals that are "as easy to check into as hotels"[6]—so phony that one of them acknowledged being unprepared to care for anyone who might really be sick.

The story includes doctors who propose unnecessary surgery, write fictional medical reports, and routinely order unneeded neck and back traction. Naturally, the system relies upon accident "victims" who lie and fake their way to settlements—often up to $10,000 in minor accidents that produced no real injuries. The goal, in fact, is settlement with the auto insurance companies. As the *Sun-Times* reported: "The lawyer, for either orchestrating or winking at the fraudulent evidence, gets a third off the top. The clinics, doctors and hospitals get the phony business. The clients get what's left, tax free."[7] Moreover, with "time lost" from work and other considerations, most settlements are three times the actual "expenses" run up by fake accident victims.

According to an unnamed personal-injury lawyer—himself involved in the swindle prior to 1980, but then caught, convicted, and disbarred—the racket involved at least 150 Chicago attorneys. He explained that an attorney with 150 such cases a year could earn $250,000—and some law offices handled up to 100 cases a week. "In Chicago," he said, "it is not a million-dollar business. It amounts into the hundreds and hundreds of millions of dollars each year." Furthermore, he claimed, "90 percent of all claims are utterly spurious."[8]

Is this difficult to believe? Working together, the *Sun-Times* and WLS-TV in Chicago sent out a team of undercover reporters to infiltrate the city's liability racket. They didn't spend years at the task—only weeks. According to the *Sun-Times*: "The reporters learned the art of swindle in the offices of 11 law firms, 4 accident 'brokers,' 9 medical clinics, 9 chiropractors, 14 physicians and 8 hospitals. Along the way, they met dozens of phony accident 'victims' posing for profit."[9] The unusual probe was conducted with the foreknowledge and cooperation of Allstate Insurance Company, a major underwriter of auto insurance policies, and the Chicago Police Department.

It is not Chicago alone that should bear such scrutiny. Los Angeles television station KNBC conducted a similar probe of the same liability racket in Southern California. Reporting the results of this investigation in 1984, the *National Underwriter*, an insurance trade journal, noted KNBC's estimate that 100 lawyers and 50 doctors and chiropractors took part in the Southern California scheme. "One chiropractor became a millionaire and acquired six Mercedes automobiles before he was convicted on a 52-count indictment and sent to federal prison," said the *National Underwriter*. A spokesman for the California Insurance Department described Southern California as "the insurance fraud capital of the world."[10]

One man interviewed by KNBC said that he had staged accidents for two years. A favorite ploy was to cruise wealthy residential areas in search of a woman backing an expensive auto out of her driveway, to cross behind her, and to get hit. The stager would then blame the woman; he picked women because, he said, they are easier to intimidate. His daily goal was six staged accidents.

One truck driver interviewed said that he realized his "accident" had been staged only when he spotted the same car he had struck involved in a fresh "accident" ten minutes later and a few blocks away.

The most common accident scam in the area, says 20th Century Insurance Company, is the "swoop and squat" maneuver, which usually involves three cars. One, of course, is the target car. Another is the "swoop" car, which makes a sudden lane change in front of the "squat" auto. The squat car then stops (squats) suddenly in front of the oncoming target car, while the swoop auto goes its merry way. The accident then becomes the "fault" of the driver of the target car, and various persons in the aggrieved squat car are ready to file phony claims.

"The occupants of the 'squat' car all file phony . . . insurance claims for nonexistent, soft tissue injuries because such injuries are subjective and difficult to verify by x-ray,"[11] notes Robert Thompson, president of 20th Century. He also says that the accident stagers prefer to avoid a police investigation of the accident. Since the police investigate only in the event of apparent injury, the stagers save their injury complaints for later, after the accident. Then they file claims for $2,500 to $4,000 a person—amounts kept small to avoid suspicion or review of the claims payments by persons in higher authority.

"It's that simple," says Thompson. "If you're not aware of a scam possibility, you'll never know the difference, except that your auto insurance rates probably will go up, and your driving record can get a black mark."[12]

In order to make people aware, and to tackle the insurance fraud head-on, Thompson's firm, the sixth largest insurer of private passenger cars in California, launched its "Operation Anti-Scam" as a community education campaign to alert the public. The tools employed by 20th Century were a speakers' bureau available to business, civic, and social organizations and a presentation that included KNBC's audiovisual clips. The insurance company also established its own investigative unit to examine suspicious accidents.

As one result, 20th Century soon discovered that the stagers backed out when they sensed an in-house investigation of their claims. In one case Thompson cited, company sleuths realized that thirteen claimants from thirteen separate accidents over a one-year period all shared the same attorney.

When 20th Century began examining the weakest cases, all thirteen were dropped.

In depositions taken from stagers, the company also learned that some insurance firms were considered "patsies" by the scam perpetrators, while others had the reputation of being "hardnosed." Whichever they were, the California scam was netting phony claimants millions of dollars a year in the early 1980s. Thompson said at the time: "Thousands and thousands of accidents are deliberately staged and unsuspecting, innocent drivers are the victims. Law enforcement officials tell us the majority of the people involved in staging accidents work in sophisticated and organized fraud rings. In many cases, the Kingpins are crooked doctors, lawyers and chiropractors."[13] (According to other sources, the riches involved in auto cases can attract organized crime, as chasers with criminal records corrupt willing lawyers, put pressure on them, refer an increasing number of corrupt cases, and up their demands to 40 or 50 percent of the lawyers' fees.)

As the KNBC-TV series noted, the stagers used disheveled old cars, called "crash cars" or "buckets," which usually were large enough to accommodate up to five passengers—all of whom were ready to submit false claims for injury. Commercial vehicles were a noted target, since they generally are well insured. They became even more of a target as the insurance firms in Southern California began to look for signs of fraud in accidents involving passenger cars.

Does such activity mean that all lawyers are dishonest? Clearly not, but attorneys who aspire to a good reputation as a profession might as well face the facts: Some attorneys *are* dishonest, and the behavior of that minority *does* give the entire profession a black eye. In a 1977 Gallup poll, for instance, respondents were asked to assess the integrity of the various professions in America. In a rating far below that given to physicians, only 26 percent of the respondents were willing to assign lawyers a high to very high standard of honesty.

In response, *The American Lawyer*, a lawyers' trade journal decided to test that low rating by taking a trumped-up accident case before a small number of negligence lawyers, "who [as a group] are, fairly or unfairly, the attorneys most often suspected of chicanery."[5]

As the journal's Jane Berentson explained, she posed as an accident victim with an obviously flawed case: "I went to 13 New York personal injury lawyers with a 'case' in which their willingness to aid and abet me in perjuring myself could produce a large contingency fee: an undetectable lie would turn a hopeless claim into a winner with potential for a big recovery."[14]

The alleged "facts" were that she had stumbled stepping off a curb at Broadway and 70th Street one evening and had fallen on her back. Nearby were barriers surrounding a Consolidated Edison construction site, "located maybe two or three feet from my accident."[15] She had been "day dreaming" when she stepped off the curb, and the construction materials had nothing to do with her alleged mishap.

A woman helped her and even accompanied her in a taxi to a hospital, where X rays taken of the "victim's" back showed no injury. For the next two months, though, her back remained a source of pain. Finally, she was placed in traction for eight days, then given a myelogram. She reported: "The diagnosis was that I had a ruptured disc and should consider an operation. But the odds weren't great. 'In your case,' the doctor explained, 'we can't guarantee your back will be better after the operation. There's a 30 percent chance it will be, but your condition may remain the same, or even get worse.'"[16]

Deciding against the operation, the victim waited at home several months, her back no better, finding it difficult to go out and look for a job and facing what now appeared to be a long-term disability. Finally, she decided to investigate the possibility of a lawsuit—and she approached thirteen randomly picked New York attorneys with her concocted story.

"The case I fabricated was not ambiguous," wrote Ms. Berentson later. "It was clear to the attorney that to have a claim I would have to perjure myself about a key fact, and that he would have to agree to help me." Since the statute of limitations allowing possible suit against the city of New York had run out, the key would be Con Ed's possible liability in the cooked-up scenario. By the "facts" Ms. Berentson related, Con Ed was *not* at fault in any way. She wrote: "At no time did I make an initial, direct offer to lie about the Con Ed construction's being the cause of my fall. But I kept emphasizing how close to my fall the construction was—and strongly implied that I was willing to shift the location of the fall slightly to make this a good case."[17]

To make a long story short, five of the thirteen lawyers Ms. Berentson approached were willing to "buy" her implication and take the case; the other eight turned her down flat. "My experiment yielded no gray areas," she said. "The dishonest lawyers picked up on my suggestion immediately; the honest ones couldn't be tempted no matter how hard I tried."[18]

Unnamed Dishonest Lawyer A didn't beat around the bush. "As it stands, you don't have a case," he said. "But if you're asking me to help fabricate a story, I can do this. All we have to do is bend the facts a little." But that would mean swearing under oath, demurred the lawyer's "aggrieved" visitor. "Everybody lies under oath," he said. "It comes down to your word against Con Ed's."

At another point he called Con Ed the "perfect" defendant. "Everybody hates Con Ed," he said, "and everybody thinks Con Ed is rich." Still utterly candid, he told Ms. Berentson, "It's up to you—whether you're up to, well, quite frankly, lying."[19]

Somewhat less frank but clear nonetheless was Dishonest Lawyer B: "The only alteration we'd have to make is to replace your vagueness about slipping on the curb with something more definite."[20]

Said Dishonest Lawyer C: "It happened on the street where Con Ed is screwing up. You get it?"[21]

Dishonest Lawyer D was on the same track. "You go into court and say you were day dreaming, and they'll throw you out," he warned. "*Something* made you fall. Something Con Ed did made you fall. Debris spilled over from the construction site. You tripped on it." The same attorney told Ms. Berentson she didn't "have to lie." No, he said, "all you have to do is shade the facts a bit. Just a little *shading* about where you fell. Everything else is fine."[22]

Finally, Dishonest Lawyer E took the view that she needed to "refresh" her memory. "As it stands, as you present the facts to me now, you have no case. But you've got a serious injury and you really need to refresh your memory."

"But I've been back to the site. . . ."

"You need to go again. If you go back there, and you find something, and then you can tell me that Con Edison construction made you fall, then, as I said before, I can help you."

Worrying that Con Ed's lawyers would grill her on the stand, Ms. Berentson expressed fear that her story would fall apart under questioning. "Leave them to me," said Dishonest Lawyer E, "I'll do all of the talking. I meet these guys in court every day and make mincemeat of them. Really, your story is very simple. You have nothing to worry about."

What about the helpful woman witness who accompanied the "victim" to the hospital in a taxi? Should *she* testify?

"Why don't you go with her to the site tomorrow," said Lawyer E. "If she'll agree with you about where you fell, so much the better. If she doesn't, then we might not want to bring her into the case at all."[23]

Lawyer A, on the same point, had asked: "Does your friend need money? Because there would be some money in this for her, too. She would be paid a fee for testifying." Lawyer B had said the friendly woman must go along with Ms. Berentson's own account, or "we don't have a case."[24]

Estimates of how much Ms. Berentson might win with her case ranged from Lawyer A's prediction of $20,000 to $30,000, or more, up to Lawyer E's anticipated award of $60,000 to $100,000—with the attorneys taking their contingency fee of about 30 percent.

The honest attorneys Ms. Berentson found were equally—and refreshingly—blunt. "You could lie, but I wouldn't be your lawyer," said one. "Look," said another, "we don't go out there and dig holes and break up pavement for our clients." Others said she didn't have a case. "People don't usually get caught for perjury," was an additional comment, "but I wouldn't get involved in a case where my client perjured himself." And finally: "No lawyer is going to help you if he knows you're lying."[25]

Unfortunately, that last declaration turned out to be a false hope, as Ms. Berentson discovered in her other visits and as the *Chicago Sun-Times* so amply revealed in its joint investigation of accident fraud with WLS-TV.

In Chicago the none-too-subtle language reported by journalists posing as accident victims was cut from the same cloth that Ms. Berentson faced on five of her New York rounds.

"You should complain to the doctor and make it sound worse than you are," explained one Chicago lawyer visited by a pair of undercover reporters pretending to be accident victims. "Tell him you can't sleep at night, you've got migraine headaches, you have dizzyness, your neck hurts and your back hurts." A short hospital stay would "help" the case by about $1,000, he counseled, but the hospital stay must be followed by outpatient treatment and a respite from work. "The more a person puts into a case, the more you get out of it," explained this attorney.[26]

Later joined by a third reporter, the first two had introduced themselves as accident victims whose shoulders and necks were still sore. One reporter said that her back hurt, too. When the lawyer asked what the third reporter's problem was, the newcomer said that his left shoulder was a bit sore and that he had been "just shook up."

According to the *Sun-Times*, "That wasn't good enough either." The lawyer said that he would put down that the third reporter had pain in his neck and back. The newspaper noted: "Because the damage to the car was so minor, [the lawyer] said that only two of his three new clients could go into the hospital and that it was up to them to decide which two it would be." He said that a hospital stay wouldn't be all that bad: "You lay there, they feed you, you flirt with the nurses."[27]

The third reporter said that he had heard of people collecting money after a train or airplane wreck, but not in the case of such a minor auto accident.

You'll never read about your case in the newspaper," said the attorney. Victims of really serious accidents "contribute their legs," he added. "You contribute a stay in the hospital."[28]

Another attorney visited by investigating reporters was, if anything, even more frank. "You've both got to go into the hospital," this lawyer told his pair of new but phony clients. "This is all just a jigsaw puzzle. When all the pieces fit together, it spells money."

One of the reporters asked if going to the hospital was absolutely necessary. "Yeah, that's a piece of the puzzle," said the lawyer. He then handed the reporter a card bearing the name of a medical clinic the reporter should visit. "I want you to complain, too. Blackouts, headaches, backaches, the whole bit."

On the way out, the reporter asked the lawyer again what to tell the doctor. "Tell him you've been blacking out, have headaches, neck and back pain, how you can hardly use your arms," said the lawyer. "Really play it up to the doctor."[29]

At the clinic, the reporter "disobeyed" his counselor and said only that his shoulder hurt. After the examination, added the *Sun-Times*, "someone at the clinic called [the lawyer], who asked to speak to [the reporter]." The lawyer then told the reporter that he wouldn't be placed in the hospital merely for a sore shoulder. "You've got to tell him [the doctor] what I told you to say."

Dutifully, the reporter went back to the same doctor the next day; this time, he said that he was feeling much worse. The *Sun-Times* noted: "The doctor welcomed the relapse and said he would hospitalize [the reporter] immediately."[30]

Meanwhile, a fresh pair of reporters appeared in the same lawyer's office as alleged passengers from the same cooked-up accident. Without inquiring about any injuries, the lawyer asked one of these reporters if he was willing to enter a hospital. The reporter at first said yes but then added that his wife would wonder why, since "she knows I'm not hurt."

The attorney didn't beat around the bush. "To make money," he said, "that's the reason. To make money—do you need it any simpler than that?" The same lawyer, according to the *Sun-Times*, once had his law license suspended for a year for settling a $1,000 personal-injury case without informing his client.[31]

The Chicago investigators also uncovered unethical practitioners in the medical profession. A chiropractor recommended by a third attorney said that he was going to be candid. (Of course, the reporter visiting the medical man wasn't injured in the slightest.) "You don't need to be in the hospital," acknowledged the chiropractor, ". . . but it makes no difference to me. The only reason you are going in the hospital is because [the attorney who referred you here] wants you in the hospital."

When the faking reporter remained silent, the chiropractor went on: "Listen, [your attorney] could [sic] care less about you or your injuries. All he is thinking about is the money."[32]

Was the chiropractor an isolated case? Apparently not, according to the *Sun-Times*. "During their investigation," said the newspaper, "undercover reporters for the *Sun-Times* and WLS-TV (Channel 7) found dozens of medical clinics, chiropractors, doctors and hospitals eager to help lawyers manufacture or exaggerate medical bills." One interesting institution was a suburban community hospital that would send a "courtesy bus" to pick up uninjured "patients" from as many as thirteen clinics in Chicago proper. Five of the lawyers and law firms exposed in the newspaper-TV series sent clients to the 47-bed facility in a residential neighborhood—described as mostly "a hospital in name only."[33]

The investigators hired a professional registered nurse to penetrate this medical facade. At their instigation, she applied for a job at the hospital. An administrator interviewing her for the job warned, "You're going to be . . . bored here because there really is nothing to do." Still, the nurse was hired.

On the second day at work, she entered the room of a patient supposedly suffering traumatic neck strain. He was doing deep knee bends. "I have to do my push-ups and calisthenics so I don't get out of shape here," he explained. A nurse accompanying the newcomer commented: "See, they're not sick at all."[34]

Another hospital staff member told the new nurse: "If we get any really sick patients here, we transfer them right out." As one resulting problem for the nurses, the patients held parties in their rooms and sometimes were rowdy. Said one nurse: "You wouldn't have this trouble if they were real patients, but you know they are not real patients." The new nurse was warned to take a guard along on her night rounds, "because of the drinking and drug problems." She expressed concern that the hospital was distributing powerful drugs just to keep the patients placated. "They love it," responded the house doctor. He had no licence to practice in Illinois, the *Sun-Times* added.

When the new nurse persisted, noting that the patients might want their drugs just to get "high," the same doctor said: "Don't bother . . . just give it."[35]

On another occasion, a 30-year old patient who was the son of an attorney's secretary told the undercover nurse that he was in the hospital because he was suing for $10,000. "My mom and my lawyer told me to come here," he said. "Now I'll just sit back and wait for the money to come."[36]

Generally, patients at the community "hospital" stayed five days and built up a bill of $1,000 to $2,000. The turnover was so frequent and X-ray procedures so haphazard that patients were discharged before their X rays became available. Some doctors at the hospital "customarily faked" their patients' records and routinely ordered unneeded pain pills and narcotics. Almost every patient had been admitted for an alleged orthopedic injury, yet this hospital had no orthopedic doctor on hand, no physical therapist, no traction equipment. Patients' beds were separated by unsanitary curtains, and the place was so infested with insects that an exterminator who was called in to take a look could only recommend burning the building down. One day, the undercover nurse saw a cockroach fall from another nurse's hair.

The investigating team found a physcian who had recently quit the facility in disgust after serving as the admitting doctor for seven months. She said that as many as 75 percent of the 800 patients she had reviewed did not require hospitalization. When she became suspicious and began discharging patients, they became rude and threatening. She later related: "They would say, 'No, my lawyer says I have to stay at least five days. If you want me to leave, I'm going to call my lawyer.'"[37]

An investigating reporter who wangled his way into the facility by the swindle pipeline found the suburban institution to be as the undercover nurse had described. He talked to almost all of the fifteen to twenty-five accident patients who were there at various times during his stay. "Only one complained about anything—a sore wrist. Most were phony neck-and-back specials, building up their case."[38] (In serious pain, though, was a woman recovering from an abortion performed at the facility.)

Although the suburban facility infested with insects might have been an extreme example, it was not alone in its free-and-easy approach to accepting patients, the *Sun-Times* said. "Checking into a hospital can be as easy as checking into a hotel," began one of the newspaper's stories. "'We wouldn't have enough hotel and motel rooms in the country to take care of their needs,' said one prominent (and honest) orthopedic specialist."[39] The *Sun-Times* reporters were "patients" in seven Chicago area hospitals, where they spent from three to six days at a cost of from $500 to $1,699 per stay. Since liability insurance companies routinely pay three times the medical bills (supposedly for the victim's "pain and suffering"), those bills could have padded insurance settlements by $1,500 to $5,100.

The same account said that the reporters met dozens of other phony accident victims and were given totally unnecessary treatments—even after some told their doctors they weren't hurt and others gave only the slightest complaints. Furthermore: "Some reporters were charged for doctors' visits never made and X-rays never taken."[40] In one case, a physician proposed surgery for correction of a shoulder separation—but, as attested by X ray and examination by other physicians, there was nothing wrong with the reporter-patient's shoulder at all.

In another aspect of the swindle game, the investigating journalists found law firms that would pay money in advance for the opportunity to represent the faking accident victims: "The law firms paid them for staying away from work and for going into a hospital to inflate the value of the case. Then they paid the reporters for referring other clients, who also were undercover reporters."

The office manager of one Chicago law firm said: "When a lawyer offers you money, you know you've got a good case. We want you to make money because the more you make, the more I make and the more this office makes." "Interviews with dozens of clients, ambulance chasers, and others," said the newspaper, "suggest the payment practice in Chicago is astonishingly widespread—even though it could mean disbarment for a lawyer."[41]

The sleaze strata, in addition to those already mentioned, also included "accident brokers," described as nonlawyers who work for themselves and settle nearly all of their cases out of court. Three such "experts" examined closely in the swindle series had graduated from their time in the streets as ambulance chasers. The newspaper noted: "Years of seeing lawyers make big money from automobile accidents taught them something—they could make it, too." If they occasionally did need an attorney for a formality such as a deposition, there were plenty to turn to. In fact, all three brokers described by the *Sun-Times* "operated out of offices that were either shared with lawyers or had the names of lawyers on the door."[42]

At the bottom of the pile remain the chasers. John and Maryann Lederer met their chaser at the scene of their minor rear-end auto accident—he was the investigating police officer, the Lederers said later. Although they told him they were unhurt, he "coaxed" them into visiting a hospital emergency room, and he followed them there in his squad car. As they were X-rayed, he telephoned a lawyer. The X rays showed no problem, but the Lederers were guided by their policeman "benefactor" to a nearby room where the alerted lawyer was waiting.

He "came on really strong," recalled Lederer, a city fireman. He told the couple that they could have their car repaired and "make some money on the side." Similar cases, he told them, had been settled for $10,000. He then gave them the name of a chiropractor he would recommend their seeing. "That would get the phony medical-bill ball rolling," explained the *Sun-Times*. The couple rebuffed the attorney. And Lederer later made it clear he didn't have high regard for a policeman who acted as a chaser. "He's short-changing the people of the city," said the firefighter. "He wasn't hired to be an ambulance chaser. He was hired to do the job of a policeman, and that's the job he should have been doing."[43]

In Chicago, as well as in Southern California, chasers stage "squat" accidents almost routinely. One policeman speculated that they stage as many as ten a day on Chicago's South Side. Favorite targets are out-of-state and expensive cars.

But, as suggested at the beginning of this chapter, ambulance chasing is by no means confined to auto accidents. In a bus accident in Chicago, said a chaser, ten persons were on the bus, but it took 25 ambulances to get all the "injured" to the hospital. A few chasers "dropping" as "victims" had joined in. And there, along with the handy referral of an accident victim to an eager lawyer, the sleaze chain begins, eventually including doctors, lawyers, medical clinics, hospitals, an apparent host of corrupt social sycophants, and even organized crime—not to overlook the often phony or vastly exaggerating victims themselves.

Minutes after the aforementioned American Airlines crash at O'Hare Airport in May 1979, said one chaser later, he recognized fifteen "fellow professionals" at the horrifying scene—looking for wallets and other items that would identify the mangled dead. A successful referral of a victim's family to a lawyer was worth $10,000 "a head," the chaser explained. "Such fees are nothing compared to the potential million-dollar settlements for families of Flight 191 victims," added the *Sun-Times*.[44]

In fact, an attorney and a former insurance investigator were later charged with soliciting two Joliet (Illinois) families whose daughters were killed in the crash: "The families said the pair employed high-pressure sales tactics." One of the mothers said later: "It just didn't seem like they cared. They were out for the money." And a father said: "They just want to fill their pockets up. . . . They don't have any feeling for anybody else."[45]

Chicago holds no monopoly, of course, on the "fix-it" racket. As indicated earlier New York City, for one, also has its share of unscrupulous attorneys and judges. In testimony before the New York State Senate's Committee on Crime and Corrections, former attorney Spencer Lader, 32, said that he earned about $1.5 million over a three-year period (1979–82) by improperly selling about a hundred tort cases to various law firms in New York City. He never appeared in court himself in regard to the personal injury cases, he said. For the most part, the suits were instituted in Brooklyn, but a few spilled over into the civil courts of Manhattan and Queens.

What Lader had to say that was specific as to his own activities has deeper implications, however, for his own activities could not have taken place without a hidden but cooperative factor—an available system of corruption. For instance, he testified that he had paid court personnel to eavesdrop on deliberating juries. Armed with knowledge of which way a jury was leaning, the informed lawyer could then decide whether to settle before the verdict came in or stick it out to the well-anticipated end.

Lader testified that he took part in the bribery of judges and in other irregularities in both medical malpractice cases and other negligence suits. He had cooperated with other lawyers "in illegal and questionable practices" to manufacture cases or to enhance the awards in legitimate suits, reported the *New York Times* in an account of his testimony.[46]

In 1983, Lader pleaded guilty to charges of defrauding several persons of more than $600,000. Sentenced to two to six years in prison on the state charges, he appealed. A federal prosecutor and the Brooklyn District Attorney's office had recommended probation, since he was cooperating with them in unrelated corruption investigations of the court system. Lader appeared before the Senate committee in January 1985 in a closed hearing that was part of the committee's investigation of the efficacy of state laws governing the illegal buying and selling of cases among lawyers. Committee Counsel Jeremiah McKenna said that Lader provided the names of twenty-one law firms to which he had referred more than a hundred cases.

Among his allegations, Lader said that he personally had paid off judges and court personnel with checks. He said that he took part in the bribery of court clerks to obtain the stamped signature of judges on phony subpoenas that gave lawyers access to confidential hospital records. With those records, the lawyers could cook up malpractice cases.

Going a step further, he made payments of up to $2,000 to staff workers at cerebral palsy rehabilitation centers for confidential patient files. The patients then were sought out and encouraged to file malpractice suits against their doctors or hospitals.

Another activity to which Lader testified was the coaching of doctors who appeared in court without ever having examined the plaintiff or his medical records. Doctors willing to testify for the plaintiff under such blind conditions were normally paid $5,000 a case, said Lader.

Members of the Senate committee apparently were startled by Lader's revelations. "You indicated clerks, court officers and judges were paid off," questioned State Senator Jeremy S. Weinstein, a Brooklyn Democrat serving on the committee. "By who? By yourself or by others?"

"By myself and others as well," was the answer.

"You said that you had proof of it by virtue of checks," pressed Weinstein. "You paid off people. You paid off judges with checks? And they accepted checks?"

Lader said yes, they had. He also said that he had given federal investigators canceled checks for the payments he had made to judges and court workers. "The jury, of course, is influenced by the judge's decisions [during trial] and other things that the judge might do improperly while he is presiding," Lader noted.

At the same hearing, Committee Counsel McKenna said that federal prosecutors would rather the committee didn't press Lader for details about the alleged courthouse corruption, "because it is under their investigation." Thus, Lader did not say how many judges he had paid off, nor did he identify the court personnel who accepted his bribes. He did name workers at cerebral palsy centers in Brooklyn and Queens who took money in exchange for confidential records. He also named several law firms that paid him in advance for sending them contingency-fee cases. Under New York law, lawyers may refer such cases, but any payment must await the outcome of the case. Lader said that he already had testified before a federal grand jury in Brooklyn "about judges being paid off."[47]

While under investigation for fraud in 1982, Lader resigned from the bar. In his later appearance before the Senate panel, he said that he was complying with a demand by federal investigators that he return his fees from all tainted cases.

The committee chairman, State Senator Christopher Mega, said that his committee also would be looking into unethical practices in malpractice and negligence cases, along with the referral practices of lawyers. Lader's testimony, he said, "is startling and cannot be ignored."[48] Staff investigators were set to work in an effort to confirm Lader's allegations.

In New York and Chicago, as elsewhere in America, there *are* honest doctors, lawyers, and accident victims—and many a personal-injury suit or settlement has good, solid evidence behind it. Vigorous enforcement of the law, a less greedy, corruptible society—such optimistic goals would, in theory, do wonders to curb the corruption. More promising for inducing change, however, would be a major alteration in the tort system, eliminating the rank opportunities for the bystanders with "gold-lust." Why can't genuine accident victims be compensated as they deserve—they and they alone?

7

The Injured Citizenry

So "successful" has been America's hard-hitting liability system in recent years that not only doctors but also midwives, day-care centers, nursing homes, small businesses, large businesses, colleges, insurance companies, public school systems, subsections of industry, and entire cities are feeling a painful pinch. Even the giant federal budget reflects the impact of the billions that now must be allocated to lawsuits.

Although their lawsuits are individual actions, liability plaintiffs and their lawyers are having a concerted impact on their own—our own—society. If tort law is to be defended as an extension of the "little man's" right to protect himself, it is ironic that his rights, in one court after another, are actually wiping out certain other rights that were once available for all. "Lawsuits' Surge Strains Budgets of Many Cities," headlined the *New York Times* one Sunday in the spring of 1985. "Explosive Growth of Lawsuits Against the U.S. Creates Concern over Potential Budget Impact," headlined the *Wall Street Journal* earlier the same year. "Sorry, Your Policy Is Cancelled" was the cover story of *Time* magazine on March 24, 1986. "Big jury awards force 10 of the 13 U.S. firms making sports helmets to halt production," said *U.S. News & World Report* in August 1985. "More than 16,000 asbestos-damage suits put giant Manville Corporation into bankruptcy court," said another story. As any newspaper reader knows, also, the pharmaceuticals giant A.H. Robins had to seek the shelter of a Chapter 11 bankruptcy after a deluge of suits arising from its Dalkon Shield intrauterine device.

"Doctors Get Out of the Delivery Game," noted *USA Today*, along with "Malpractice Makes for Unhappy Obstetricians" in another headline the same day. "Drunken-Driving Suits Aiming at Third Parties," warned the *Washington Post*. "Malpractice Insurers Are Ill," proclaimed *Newsweek*. "Can Medicine Rely on the Rules of the Marketplace?" questioned the *New*

York Times in a piece noting that fewer drug companies were willing to make vaccines—a decrease blamed, in large part, on lawsuits instigated by the rare victims of side effects.

"The Tort Explosion" was *The New Republic's* headline for a more general discussion. On another occasion in 1985, a *New York Times* headline was "Businesses Change Ways in Fear of Lawsuits." The implication might have been a positive one—until one notes that in the first example cited in the article, the businessman simply went out of business. Like many others in various professions and occupations, he could no longer obtain liability insurance as protection against possible lawsuits. The businessman was Charles Shultz, creator of the comic strip *Peanuts;* the business he closed down was a public ice-skating rink he owned in Santa Rosa, California.

Shultz presumably was able to fall back on other assets, but not every businessman would be so fortunate. For many, if not most, a proprietorship would be their sole venture, and shutting down could mean financial disaster. And in late 1985, Schultz was not alone. Owners of 100 to 200 ice rinks across the country were struggling to obtain liability insurance at any price, according to James C. Goodale, owner of Manhattan's Sky Rink. Thus, an entire class of entrepreneurs, to say nothing of their ice-skating faithful, must pay an undeserved penalty because of lawsuit risk.

Society as a whole, of course, may not need ice skating all that much, but society in the aggregate might be surprised at the many ways, both visible and insidious, in which the "tort explosion" has had an impact. In Houston, for instance, many ministers have stopped making house calls for fear of lawsuits. Instead, they will counsel troubled parishioners at church offices only. Across the country, too, real estate brokers, wary of suits by disgruntled home buyers or sellers, require that the sellers provide disclosure of any possible flaws in their property. The real estate brokers have seen their legal expenses triple in recent years because of lawsuits.

Public school officials in Redding, California, found no solace in the fact that a 19-year-old youth who was injured in 1982 on school property was a would-be burglar. Admittedly, he was on a lark—trying to take a floodlight off a high school roof. He suffered a paralyzing injury when he fell through a skylight. Fearing the possibility of an even higher award by a jury, the insurance carrier in the case settled for a $260,000 outright payment, plus $1,500 a month.

Soon after, California's beach cities were hit by half a dozen lawsuits on the heels of a $6 million award to a swimmer injured at a town beach in Newport Beach, California. He had dived into the ocean and struck a hidden sandspit, seriously injuring himself; his lawyer argued that the underwater obstacle should have been marked in warning.

"It's hard to resist not suing when the news is constantly filled with the latest wrinkle in lawsuits," remarked Charles W. Terranova, headmaster of a Montessori school in Scituate, Massachusetts, in 1985.[1] His school had just signed up for an expensive liability insurance policy that protected it against lawsuits.

In Washington, D.C., the city's corporation counsel had to ask the city council for more money in May 1985, two-thirds of the way through the budgetary fiscal year, to pay for settlements and awards stemming from lawsuits against the District government. Her $5 million payout fund was nearly exhausted, said Counsel Inez Smith Reid. "The whole problem of lawsuits is burgeoning," she commented. "Cities nationwide are experiencing a veritable explosion in municipal liability."[2]

Her plea for more money came the day after a local jury had awarded $250,000 in damages to a 15-year-old girl who, five years earlier, had been lured from an unsupervised classroom in a public school and then sexually assaulted.

Reid cited a "gradual erosion" of special defenses traditionally available to governmental defendants in liability cases. She said: "This office will continue to devote its resources to minimizing recoveries against the District and will continue to seek reversals of unjustifiably inflated jury awards. However, the general tendency to higher verdicts is a fact of life which must be dealt with."[3]

In the area of city finance, just as in the case of big business, most of us tend to view the mounting total of personal injury awards as somebody else's bill to pay, not ours. Even when we think the issue through, it may seem to be a small matter on an individual basis. What does it cost to pay the injured party—a few cents per taxpayer? So what's the fuss? Pay the man (or woman or child), and let's get on with life—or some such reaction.

By the mid-1980s, though, some cities, stung by multimillion-dollar awards, were forced to cut back city services—a penalty for *all* their citizens. In 1985, experts in the field said that the spiraling costs to taxpayers had tripled in just five years.

Indeed, the Advisory Commission on Intergovernmental Relations warned Congress in April 1985 that such legal judgments were looming as one of the most serious financial problems facing American cities, especially smaller cities. Many had been forced to borrow money through long-term revenue bonds, traditionally a city's or state's source for capital (one-time construction) needs, not operating expenses. A few cities had even gone into bankruptcy—Bay St. Louis, Missouri; Wapanucka, Oklahoma; South Tucson, Arizona. "Juries find towns a deep pocket," explained H.I. Manke, assistant town attorney for Hamden, Connecticut. "When we go to trial, we've already got one foot in the hole."[4]

This is a far cry from the days, not so very long ago, when governmental entities enjoyed "sovereign immunity"—a residue of the old common law that once held that the king can do no wrong. Now it seems the king can hardly do anything right. In Los Angeles, a jury awarded $3 million to the victim of a crime because the police allegedly left the scene *before* the crime took place. In South Tucson, Arizona, a police officer was accidentally shot by a fellow police officer and was left paralyzed. In the suit that followed, the injured policeman, Roy Garcia, was awarded $3.59 million. That 1980 award was later reduced to $3 million. South Tucson, a city of 6,500, went into bankruptcy trying to pay the huge bill. With about half of the money going to his lawyer, the city raised most of a $1.69 million lump-sum payment for Garcia by issuing revenue bonds and using city property worth $1 million. The city recovered from its bankruptcy status, but promised to pay Garcia another $300,000 over the next ten years.

In hard-hit California, meanwhile, the lawsuit binge has burgeoned. Mayor William J. Carroll of Vacaville, president of the California League of Cities, says that the judgments "represent a ludicrous abuse of justice when government is brought in on flimsy bases and taxpayers are forced to pay the bill."[5] A League survey of 162 cities, a third of all those in California, found that in 1984 they paid more than $19 million in liability claims and faced others totaling $210 million. In the aggregate, they had spent more than $15 million defending themselves. The League report said: "California's local governments are closing libraries and recreation facilities and cutting back police and fire services to pay the cost of this litigation explosion."[6]

Is it conceivable that the next escalation in litigation will find plaintiffs suing bankrupt cities for a lack of police or fire protection they couldn't provide because of the impact of earlier court awards? Almost anything seems possible these days, even that.

"Say a pedestrian is hit by a car," says California State Senator John F. Foran, a Democrat proposing legislation to place a cap on municipal liability. "If the city where the accident occurs is even found to be 1 percent responsible and the driver is uninsured, the city can be stuck paying all the damages, usually in the millions of dollars. This money comes out of the deep pockets of the taxpayers."[7]

Like private parties, cities often obtain protective insurance to cover liability costs. Nowadays, though, it's become a question of how they can afford the rapidly escalating premium costs—a result of high and proliferating court awards. In 1985, Montrose, Colorado—population around 9,000—was billed $182,000, a rather sharp rise from the $46,500 tab of the year before. In New Jersey, meanwhile, companies insuring municipalities cut back their coverage for all after one town suffered a $17.6 million judgment in a toxic waste case. In that instance, Jackson Township was ordered to pay for alleged negligence in the operation of a landfill containing toxic chemicals. Ninety-seven families sued, claiming that the contaminants leaked into their well water. Toxicity and environmental claims of this sort can be extremely expensive because of the potential numbers of victims involved and the staggering costs of cleaning up. Since that decision, reported the *New York Times* in 1985, "companies that insure municipal governments in New Jersey have curbed their coverage of such perils."[8]

Across the country, reported the same article, "officials in many cities . . . said their insurance costs tripled or quadrupled in the past year or so as a result of a surge in successful lawsuits." According to Joel Cogen, executive director of Connecticut's Conference of Municipalities: "Suddenly it's become very difficult to get insurance, and the rates have gone way up."[9] Adds Timothy A. Greer, a consultant to communities seeking reduced insurance costs: "Small towns just don't have the money for those kinds of payments."[10]

"The money [to pay for skyrocketing increases in damage awards and litigation] has to come from somewhere, and that somewhere is from the taxpayers," according to Joseph Fiore, president of the Professional Insurance Agents of Connecticut, a trade group.[11]

Harrison Goldin, the New York City comptroller, stated that the city was spending $140 million in 1985 to settle claims, an amount equal to the city's cost of running the Parks or Health Departments. He called rising insurance costs "a hemorrhage that will threaten vital services."[12]

On the federal government level, it's much the same story, although Uncle Sam often is tougher to sue successfully and doesn't need to carry protective insurance. With the new latitudes seemingly allowed by the courts these days, even the elephantine bureaucracy feels the pinprick of the individual suit more often than in the past. In New England, for instance, three lobster fishermen drowned when their boats were caught in an unexpected storm. Their families sued the National Weather Service, the negligence claim being that the NWS should have repaired a faulty weather buoy that might have helped predict the storm's imminence. A federal trial court agreed. An intermediate appellate court has reversed the verdict, but a further appeal to the U.S. Supreme Court seems likely.

The pole-ax that really stuns the elephant in Washington, however, is mass-disaster litigation. Citizens in Utah, for instance, recall the government's aboveground atomic tests in the 1950s as big flashes lighting up the entire sky. Helen Jolley of Washington, Utah, saw them; then she saw her 13-year old son, Sheldon, die of cancer in 1959. There were other cancer deaths in the rural communities near the Nevada test site, and nine persons, Mrs. Jolley among them, sued. In May 1954, a federal judge in Salt Lake City ruled that radioactive fallout had been a "substantial factor" in the cancer deaths and that the government had been negligent in its warnings to area residents. The total award for all nine plaintiffs was $2.7 million.

Even that sum would seem minor in comparison to the huge federal budget, but the rationale behind the decision has federal officials worried. "The reasoning could apply to so many cases," explained a government attorney.[13] Going further, Wayne Vance of the Justice Department's civil division worried that the ruling would be "an invitation to people who have cancer from unknown causes to come forward and file radiation cases."[14] By early 1985, in fact, more than 1,000 radiation fallout cases were pending, and the government's potential liability in them ranged from hundreds of millions to even billions.

Overall, Uncle Sam became heavily involved in the lawsuit stampede in the mid-1980s. By the end of fiscal year 1985, Vance's civil division faced 54,000 cases, with claims amounting to $140 billion. Even though these are just the amounts *claimed*—and they are often exaggerated—for the federal budget planner, they are obviously daunting sums. Worse yet, the Justice Department's various other divisions—tax, civil rights, lands—were involved in defending Uncle Sam against "tens of thousands of other suits," reported the *Wall Street Journal* in early 1985.[15]

The potential sums must be considered a "budget wild card," noted the *Journal*. Neither the executive branch nor the legislative branch can plan or approve the "wild card" in advance. "Courts can do things in a moment that it would take Congress years to do," notes tort law expert Victor Schwartz. "Millions and possibly billions of dollars can change hands without one day of congressional hearings."[16]

If class action is the blow that really hurts, the toxic-exposure variety can be a knockout. "We're seeing a whole new type of class action," explained Richard Willard, acting assistant attorney general for the civil division, in

1985. "It isn't like someone getting run over by the postman's truck."[17] In the asbestos area alone, added the *Wall Street Journal* in early 1985:

> So many suits have been filed in recent years [against the federal government] that government attorneys have had trouble keeping track. There are currently about 2,800 cases pending involving claims of $12.2 billion; the figures are expected to rise to 9,400 cases involving $18 billion by the end of the fiscal year.... To cope, the [Justice] department is now handling all asbestos litigation from Washington and has increased the number of lawyers working exclusively on asbestos cases to 35, up from six in 1982.[18]

As is well known by now, asbestos is the insulating and fireproofing material blamed for potentially fatal lung problems. (We'll have more to say on the litigation against asbestos manufacturers in chapter 9). "Some 30,000 [asbestos related] lawsuits have been filed, and experts predict 50,000 more, with total claims exceeding 40 billion dollars," reported *U.S. News & World Report* in mid-1985.[19]

The recent asbestos litigation may be likened to an iceberg that surfaced suddenly; thousands worked with the insulating material for years before its identification as a hazardous substance. Many of the suits against Johns-Manville and other asbestos producers come from Navy shipyard workers of the World War II era who used the material for fireproofing panels. But asbestos suits against Uncle Sam come primarily from asbestos producers themselves. They argue they built the Navy's ships to government specification and thus Uncle Sam should foot the bill for the aggrieved victims of asbestos disease. If the courts should rule that the government is liable in that sense, warns tort expert Schwartz, "Katy, bar the door."[20]

Today, not only government but also the most innocuous of institutions around us are fair game for lawsuits. Even colleges have been hit by the ripple effect; they face the same insurance problems as many professionals and manufacturers because of liability risks.

The insurance company for small Hood College in Frederick, Maryland, was pulling back its coverage in 1985, apparently because the company had lost its coverage from a European reinsurer. Judith Robinson, head of the New York brokerage firm that had negotiated Hood's coverage, said that college insurers were "getting hit by claims across the board." Besides the fact that suits can threaten a school's endowment, insurers that are willing to stay in the business of college coverage have raised their premiums drastically. "Only a few years ago," says Robinson, "colleges were a perfectly clean risk. Nobody sued churches or synagogues or colleges. Now all that's changed."[21]

It certainly has, and she might have added day-care centers to the list. With more than 50 percent of American mothers of preschool children enlisted in the nation's work force these days and 8 million children placed in preschool or day-care settings, the insurance for the children's caretakers suddenly has dried up or become exorbitantly expensive. Insurance brokers who sell day-care centers their liability coverage say that it's been sharply reduced in reaction to publicity over alleged sexual abuse of children at a few centers. The higher cost of the insurance that is still available reflects insurer worries that cases of physical abuse "may go undetected for years," says James Chastain, professor of insurance at Howard University in Washington, D.C.

The impact is felt in two ways. Jean Weaver, day-care coordinator for the YWCA in Baltimore, reported that the price for liability coverage in her program rose by 212 percent in 1985. In Orange, California, Diane Beverly was forced to close her preschool in 1985 after twenty-three years of operation with no lawsuits or major accidents. Her insurance was canceled. As one result of the crisis for day-care centers, the House Select Committee on Children, Youth and Family held hearings on the issue in mid-1985. Its chairman, Representative George Miller (D.-Calif.) said: "Child care centers, family care homes, Head Start programs and resource and referral agencies report that their liability policies are not being renewed, that premiums have become prohibitive, that coverage for child abuse claims is unavailable and that policies are being canceled with little or no notification."[22] As the Insurance Information Institute's West Coast vice-president, John McCann, recently said, insuring such institutions "was once the safest, nicest, easiest insurance a company could offer."[23] This was once true, but no longer—as in so many other areas.

As McCann also said, the broad-front assault on insurance liability in better-known areas, such as medical malpractice and product defects, has sharply reduced the insurance industry's surplus, upon which new coverage is based. Others in the industry say that after a few cases of alleged sexual molestation in preschool settings made headlines, the risk factor made any day-care center far less attractive to insurers. This is unfortunate not only for the operators of those centers but also for their clientele. "Eventually, it's the parents who are going to have to pay for the increased costs; there is nobody else who can do it," says Debbie Wehbe, insurance chairman of the Pre-School Association of California. The added financial burden will pass to mothers "who are working not because they want to, but because they have to," she adds. In many cases, though, the same mothers must scramble to find a replacement for the preschool centers that have been forced out of business altogether.[24]

In the public school systems for older children, the cost situation is hardly any better, although the public schools are not likely to go out of business. What they *are* likely to do—what they apparently *must* do these days—is pay more and more precious tax dollars to cover themselves. Consider the following, in the state of Virginia alone in 1985:

> Property insurance premiums for the city schools of Norfolk shot up from $69,500 in 1984 to $147,600 in 1985, despite a widening of the deductible gap from $5,000 to $50,000.
>
> In Fredericksburg, there was a liability jump from $900 to $8,000—more than 750 percent.
>
> In Roanoke County, where liability insurance cost $9,900 in 1984, bids received in 1985 ranged from $63,000 to more than $97,000.
>
> In Caroline County, school superintendent William C. Asbury said that premiums "tripled and quadrupled overnight." Caroline paid $30,274 for its overall insurance package in 1984; in 1985, the same package would cost $131,906. "If it continues to spiral upward," said Asbury, "we're going to have to look at other options."[25]

Interesting, too, was the notation by School Superintendent L. Robert McDaniel in nearby Spotsylvania County: "We haven't had any big claims, but our premiums have gone up, partly to help cover claims for lawsuits and accidents in school systems all over the county."[26]

In rural Brunswick County, Virginia, meanwhile, the athletic department at Brunswick High sells ads in its football programs to raise funds for insurance premiums on the school's football players. Increasing premium costs are rendering the ads too expensive for some of the local merchants, however.

As noted by Virginia's insurance commissioner, James M. Thomson, the insurance companies are calling the shots. "Three years ago [1982] you had a buyer's market," he said. "Today, it's a seller's market."[27] The insurance companies left in the market are more than simply selective, adds another industry expert, Richard L. Fisher, vice-president of Industrial Insurance Management Corporation, an insurance consulting firm in Richmond, Virginia. "There are so few companies left that they can name their own price," he explains.[28] Still another Virginia school superintendent, Jerry Austin of

Mecklenburg County, makes the point that large punitive judgments against a school system actually punish the people living in that school district—in higher taxes—rather than the person who caused the injury.

Big business, of course, has been the traditional "enemy" in the turbulent world of tort law, and big business indeed has been shaken by the recent trend toward large and frequent judgments. "Companies at their highest levels are becoming more conscious of the litigation threat," notes Joseph Fiksel of the Arthur D. Little consulting firm.[29]

The first million-dollar award in a personal injury suit came in 1962. In 1970, there were eight at that threshold or higher, according to Jury Verdict Research, Inc., of Solon, Ohio. In 1975, there were 26; in 1980, 134; and by now there are over 400 annually (granted that these are trial verdicts—often reversed or scaled down on appeal).

One supposed reason for the explosion in product liability proceedings has been the shift away from the standard requiring proof of negligence to more experimental law "created" by judges and juries in a crazy-quilt pattern of state courts across the country—all dating from the 1960s. And one reason for that shift, in turn, was the perception in a world grown more and more complex that it was becoming too difficult to pinpoint just why the defective product failed. "The real rationale of strict liability is that people cannot always prove negligence even when it's there," says consumer advocate Jay Angoff of Congress Watch.[30] The replacement has been more "creative" law, providing grounds other than strictly provable negligence, and a plethora of rulings throughout the fifty states that gradually percolate through to national-level consciousness and thus sometimes take the unwary business defendant by surprise. Victor Schwartz, of the Product Liability Alliance, which represents the insurance industry and other defendant groups, is one who argues that liability rules now vary so widely from state to state that companies shipping their products from one state to another "don't know what the rules are."[31]

For small firms especially, but even for a few of the nation's biggest firms, the cost of liability rulings—and their defense—can have a major, sometimes disastrous impact. Less obvious, perhaps, is the stultifying effect that not only drives some firms *out* of business but also prevents others from going *into* new business. For example, the FMC Corporation not long ago considered production of precision bearings for helicopter rotors. The company backed off, however, because the projected profits to be gained failed to offset the liability risk in the event of one or more helicopter crashes. Yet, simply stated, if society is to have helicopters—for any number of purposes—*someone* has to make the precision bearings for the rotors. "As a lawyer and as a businessman, it's awfully difficult to project or forecast for your client," says John F. Schmutz, senior vice-president and general counsel at E.I. du Pont de Nemours & Company. "You tend to shy away from things that really would benefit society if you didn't shy away from them."[32]

8

Medical Malpractice's Malpractice

MIDWIVES have come upon hard times, and the alleged villain is insurance—malpractice insurance. "It is a crisis," says Edith Wonnell, director of the Birthing Center of Delaware in Wilmington. "This could almost wipe out an entire professional group."[1]

The real villain, though, is said to be the spate of lawsuits plaguing the entire health care apparatus of the country. Although they are sued far less than doctors, the midwives of the country have nonetheless been caught up in the crunch. A third or more of the 2,500 nurse-midwives in practice as of mid-1985 had been notified that their malpractice insurance was to be withdrawn. "The real loss," says Ms. Wonnell, "is that nurse-midwives across the country are largely caring for the poor. Obstetricians won't be picking up the care of these patients."[2]

One reason they won't is the fact that many obstetricians simply aren't around any more. In Molokai, Hawaii, for instance, expectant mothers must board an airplane for Honolulu about a week before their expected delivery. They stay with friends or relatives or make other arrangements while they await their babies' births at University of Hawaii Medical Center. They cannot stay in Molokai because its four physicians gave up obstetrics when faced with that ubiquitous villain—$24,000 a year in premiums for malpractice insurance.

The doctors of Molokai are part of a disturbing trend that has seen physicians all over the country drop their obstetrics practice in favor of early retirement, the practice of gynecology, or some entirely different pursuit. Everywhere these days there seems to be evidence of what the medical profession calls the second malpractice crisis. For the most part, the focus is on higher insurance rates, but behind those rates, at the bottom of the crisis, are the personal injury lawsuits that, fairly or unfairly, have brought doctors to bay. The effects in some instances are predictable and visible—obstetricians dropping out; in some instances, they are less apparent, more insidious, and yet far-reaching.

"The worst aspect of this crisis . . . is the harm that it has done to the patient-doctor relationship," says Dr. Richard H. Schwarz, chairman of obstetrics and gynecology at the State University of New York's Downstate Medical Center in Brooklyn. "It has increased the tension, which is a shame, because obstetrics-gynecology used to be known as the most pleasant specialty in medicine."[3]

New York state has been among the areas hit hardest by the crisis, but the ripple effect is widespread; the complaints are much the same everywhere. "I'll tell you why I quit after ten years of delivering babies," says Dr. David A. Ronk of Norman, Oklahoma. "It just got to be too much hassle for the return. It's not just the disruption of your life 24 hours a day. It's a whole atmosphere of confrontation now between doctors and patients. We believe someone must always be at fault. We're suing car makers. Why not baby makers?"[4]

Not only the adversarial edge but also high expectations for medicine's wondrous technology have had an impact. "There's an attitude that says, 'We're going to have fewer babies, so we want a perfect baby,'" according to Dr. Maurice N. Courie of Raleigh, North Carolina.[5] He dropped his obstetrics practice after nineteen years of delivering babies; his malpractice insurance premiums, which were $4,500 in 1983, had advanced to $13,000 in 1985. "When you deliver a baby today," adds Dr. Theodore Loring, another twenty-year veteran of obstetrics: "Parents expect it to come out perfectly. Unfortunately it doesn't always turn out that way. Twenty years ago it was considered an act of God. Today there are no more acts of God. They expect you should have been able to do something." Amazingly, among the things that doctors *can* do these days is nurse along an infant born at only one and a half pounds and see it live, notes Loring. "God only knows what that baby will turn out to be. And if there is something wrong, even 18 years down the road, they can sue you for millions."

Although doctors hailed into court are sometimes guilty of malpractice, often they are not. As Loring notes, the latter instance is no cause for peace of mind. "You may have documentation to defend yourself," he says, "but you still go through hell for one, two, three years of depositions and hearings. And you may win. But by then you've already lost."[6]

American health care providers pay billions of dollars a year for their malpractice insurance. The most expensive single area for the physician apparently is Long Island, the suburban community that stretches eastward from Manhattan Island. There, the obstetrician pays $55,000 a year for a million dollars in insurance coverage. Neurosurgeons, also at high risk in our "let's sue 'em" society of today, pay $101,000.

Why Long Island? The reasons are a high-density population, many couples wanting children, the sophistication to engage attorneys, and "the inclination to sue," says an insurance underwriter for a New York-based malpractice insurance group.[7] As a matter of perception, it may be significant, too, that people think doctors make a lot of money. In big, bustling New York, it's thought that they must *really* rake it in—a perception that that is fairly accurate but relative. In New York state, the average doctor's gross income in the mid-1980s was $168,300 a year; his net income was $95,000. The average physician in New York spent about 10 percent of his gross earnings on malpractice insurance premiums—on the average, $17,000 annually. These figures come from a study by the state's medical society that incorporated comparative statistics from nine other states. According to those comparisons, said the New York State Medical Society, New York's doctors paid the highest percentage of income for malpractice insurance and yet ranked near the bottom in net take-home earnings. Doctors in Florida, by comparison, earned the highest net income—$134,200 a year. Of their average gross income, set at $241,200, they spent 6.6 percent on malpractice insurance.

As one result of the malpractice crisis, New York and other high-premium areas are losing more than the services of the obstetricians who switch to gynecology only. They are also losing the services of both established and brand-new doctors who simply go elsewhere to reestablish or begin their practices. In some cases, the departing practitioners become staff members of health maintenance organizations to pool insurance costs. Less than 25 percent of the new doctors completing their specialty residencies in New York remain there to open a practice, says Dr. Stephen A. Gettinger of the American College of Obstetricians and Gynecologists. The new OB-GYN specialists may have to assign 90 percent of their first-year gross earnings to insurance costs—if they stay in New York to practice. Dr. Ivan K. Strausz, a Manhattan obstetrician-gynecologist, writes in the *New York Times:*

> Consider a scenario. Newcomers, who are still paying off debts accumulated in medical school, will not enter practice in New York City because of overhead costs. Many established physicians will retire as the simplest way out of an unbearable situation. Others, unable to pay escalating premiums, will be forced

out. Thus, the number of physicians will diminish drastically. Those remaining may accept fewer patients and attempt to practice "flawless" medicine—as if each case were going to court. This will mean more tests, more consultations, and more hospital admissions.[8]

In short, Strausz and many others who are perturbed by the trend of liability law in the world of medicine foresee a growing exodus by the most experienced doctors, a smaller number of new doctors entering the high-risk specialties, and the advent of "defensive medicine" as a matter of routine practice. "Patients may expect sharp increases in fees charged by those [remaining] physicians who in effect will have a monopoly," says Strausz. They may expect higher fees—and a lot of tests. He adds: "If you have chronic headaches, it may cost $2,000 for high-technology scans and a neurologist's reassurance that there is no brain tumor or other serious disease. Simple prenatal care may be available not for $2,000 or $3,000 but for $5,000 or, some years later, $10,000. In effect, fees will be tied to insurance costs."[9]

Doctors assert that the malpractice crisis, reaching far beyond the doctors themselves, eventually will touch anyone who needs a doctor—eventually, all of us. And it will not only affect our pocketbooks. Doctors also point to the wear and tear of the extra, sometimes unnecessary tests that gun-shy physicians are already ordering for their patients.

Consider the impact—physical, emotional, financial—on women, especially young, child-bearing women. They are the victims of a system gone beyond all reasonable bounds. Either they will be deprived of doctor services—as in the case of the expectant mothers from Molokai—or they may well have to pay much more for the services available. The billions of dollars a year that health care providers nationwide pay for their malpractice insurance, like any other overhead cost, is sought to be passed on to patients as added costs in their billings. In a 1985 New York state study of 798 obstetrician-gynecologists, 81 percent reported that they raised their fees (16 percent said that they gave up delivering babies, too).[10] According to another survey, conducted by the American College of Obstetricians and Gynecologists, more than half of the 1,900 doctors questioned had raised their fees two or more times from 1981 to 1983. As another cost item for patients, 75 percent of the 1,900 physicians said that they order more tests as protection against possible lawsuits. "Professional liability is the most serious problem facing our specialty," said Dr. William T. Mixson of Coral Gables, Florida, newly installed president of the organization at the time. "It is a problem of crisis proportions throughout the country because one out of four obstetrician-gynecologists has been sued, and awards of $1 million are not uncommon."[11]

In New York alone, the Medical Liability Mutual Insurance Company, a so-called "bedpan" insurance group formed by doctors to protect themselves, faced 420 claims against obstetrician-gynecologists in the ten years from 1975 to 1985. It paid out a staggering $79 million in seventy-five of those cases. "There are still 116 claims pending, so that the costs may be even higher," said company spokesperson Shirley Connell in 1985. "Although obstetrician-gynecologists win more than 70 percent of the suits, the cost to defend them is staggering: an average of $19,700 per claim."[12]

Nationwide, the number of malpractice suits against obstetricians had risen from 5 suits for every 100 such specialists in 1975 to 16 suits per 100 in 1983. The reported figures for the number of malpractice suits against every 100 doctors of any kind were 8 in 1983, a jump from just 3.3 in 1978.

Considering those statistics, it's no wonder that women are feeling the impact. "Women across the nation are finding that the availability of health care has decreased dramatically since 1980 because of the rising cost of professional liability insurance, the increasing number of lawsuits and higher court awards," reported the *New York Times* in 1985.[13] In New York, where insurance rates are high, the average obstetrician's fee for a normal delivery was approximately $1,800 in mid-1985, compared to around $800 in a small, low-rate city such as Parkersburg, West Virginia.

Not only delivery fees but other new practices have an impact on the woman patient. More than forty members of the American College of Obstetricians and Gynecologists interviewed at the college's convention in May 1985 said that they were cutting back to low-risk practice and referring patients needing surgery to specialists based at major hospitals. They were practicing "defensive medicine"—ordering more and more test procedures to back up their own diagnoses. According to Dr. James S. Todd, senior deputy executive vice-president of the American Medical Association, many specialists obtain second and third opinions before operating, and many doctors also spend extra time keeping additional records—"so many malpractice cases boil down to whether the doctor paid attention to some mechanical detail, such as making a notation on a patient's chart."[14]

Of course, it's impossible to say offhand whether a given instance of defensive medicine is a good or bad thing. Defensive driving is supposed to be a good thing, so why not defensive medicine, ask some critics of medicine. But in an age of skyrocketing medical costs, the fact that doctors are ordering more and more tests that they consider necessary for legal, not medical, reasons is surely a cause of concern.

Dr. Schwarz of the Downtown Medical Center in Brooklyn foresees fewer medical students choosing the OB-GYN specialty. That means that women in the future may be even more hard-pressed to find proper care. "I believe the changes we have seen so far are only the tip of the iceberg," says Schwarz.[15] Adds OB-GYN practitioner Strausz in neighboring Manhattan: "Million-dollar payments inevitably will bankrupt insurers, physicians and hospitals." Clearly, he says, "the quality of medical care can often be improved, but this does not justify honing the 'art' of suing doctors to the point that the medical system risks being undermined by silver-tongued lawyers and sympathetic juries."[16]

If women as a class are affected by the malpractice crisis, and doctors are, too, then obviously so are insurers. As one-third of an interdependent circle, they must survive if doctors are to have the ability to compensate for injuries in the course of medical treatment so that victims of adverse results of health care can receive helpful compensation. The system must provide not only for women but for other patients suffering the vicissitudes of medical accident. And yet insurers, too, insist that they have been reeling under the malpractice blows of recent years.

Included among the hard-hit have been the so-called "bedpan" insurance co-ops created by the doctors themselves. Historians of the malpractice phenomenon in twentieth-century America refer to the "first malpractice crisis"; it was during that period, the mid-1970s, that doctors in many states got together and formed their own insurance mutuals to replace the commercial insurers that were abandoning the market. It seemed to be an attractive idea, one often sponsored by a medical society. It gave the doctors their insurance coverage, and the rates charged supposedly wouldn't be all that bad, since the "bedpan" mutuals weren't in business to make money. By the mid-1980s, around forty such mutuals held an estimated 30 percent of the market in medical malpractice insurance.

By then, though, the second great crisis had struck, and even the nonprofit mutuals were reeling under the impact. In New York, the Medical Liability Mutual Insurance Company (MLMIC), insurer for 35 percent of the state's doctors, was reported in the spring of 1985 to be $750 million short of the amount necessary to pay future claims. "In states like Florida, Michigan and Illinois," according to *Newsweek*, others were "tottering toward insolvency."[17]

A major reason was the explosion in malpractice suits that made the crisis of the 1970s seem mild by comparison. Contributing to the "bedpan" circle's headache, though, was competition from among their own—new "bedpans" created by "low-risk" practitioners, such as the family physician, while leaving the high-risk specialties, such as neurosurgeons and obstetricians, to the original mutual insurers.

Among the commercial insurers, St. Paul Fire and Marine Insurance Company of St. Paul, Minnesota, is by far the largest, with a 15 percent share of the malpractice insurance market as of 1985. Its nearest commercial competitor held only about a 4.3 percent share of the market. All together, the "bedpan" mutuals formed by both doctors and hospitals held about 60 percent of the market.

Hard-hit in the first great malpractice crisis, St. Paul considered dropping out of the market entirely, and it did pull out of more than a dozen states, remaining in twenty-eight. Ten years later, it still wouldn't enter supposedly hostile regulatory climates, such as those in New York, Massachusetts, New Mexico, Rhode Island, and New Hampshire. But the company did stay in the malpractice business, one enabling factor being its switch in 1975 from the "occurrence" type of policy to a "claims-made" coverage.

This switch involves a change from policies that insure the physician forever against claims arising from treatments rendered this year (an "occurrence" policy) to policies that insure the physician against claims that arise this year from treatments rendered in the past (a "claims-made" policy). Nothing illustrates the chaos of the present liability system better than the change whereby insurance companies—supposedly expert in predicting risks and collecting premiums to cover them—say to their insureds, in effect, "We have no idea what the risks in future years will be from our insureds' acts done this year. We won't cover those risks but will rather shift them to our insureds who in future years will have to procure insurance for those risks." By requiring a doctor to forecast his future liabilities and to buy insurance later to cover those costs, a claims-made policy shifts the most unpredictable risks to insureds, who are far less able to predict and prepare for those risks than their insurance companies. What this also probably means as a practical matter is that the typical doctor, far from setting aside reserves this year to pay for future claims arising from this year's services, will be paying in future years (and then forcing his patients to pay) for the liability arising from his services rendered in past years—a sort of deficit financing, with the concomitant problems this presents to doctors and their families on retirement or death.

Even with the new policies, the claims arrive at St. Paul's corporate offices at an average of fourteen a day; as of early 1985, St. Paul insured 57,000 doctors, 100,000 nurses, and 1,500 hospitals in forty-four states. Although new claims come in faster than the old ones can be processed, paid, or refused, about two-thirds result in no reimbursement, say St. Paul officials. Still—and quite apart from the expenses involved in defending and defeating claims—those that result in payment, voluntarily or at the prod of litigation, have become more and more expensive on a per-case ratio. St. Paul's first $1 million payout came in 1975 in a neurology malpractice case. Ten years later, Norman Schindler, medical liability claims officer for St. Paul's, was saying, "We're seeing $1 million verdicts or settlements every week now." Even that incidence, he said, might be conservative. "I've got a case on my desk where our people are recommending we offer $2 million."[18]

The $2 million he cited fell short, in fact, of a settlement the company had reached shortly beforehand—its largest ever—$6 million. And that sum was agreed to in part because of a $15 million award granted by the courts of the state in which the $6 million case arose. "Frequency and severity are up," said Schindler. "We're seeing more claims and we're seeing claims that are going to cost more dollars. We find it difficult to estimate how a jury is going to react to any given incident. We found 10 years ago that we could estimate better whether a doctor or patient would win a case, and if a doctor lost how much the jury award would be."[19]

It is not that all juries are out to gouge the doctors and their insurers. Schindler recalled the case of a brain-damaged infant on whose behalf compensation was sought from an obstetrician. "We evaluated it and saw a potential award of $600,000, and we offered $600,000," said Schindler. "It was refused. We went to trial and tried it for four weeks, and the jury came back after three days with no award."[20]

St. Paul began its medical malpractice coverage in the 1930s, when only a cad would sue the friendly (but sometimes bumbling) family doctor. Times (and claims) obviously have changed. "Everyone feels that we have made so many strides [in medicine] that if we go into a hospital and something goes wrong, it has to be somebody's fault and someone will pay," says Joseph Nardi, president of St. Paul's medical services division.[21]

His colleague Schindler explains further: "We used to have just wrongful death. Now we're seeing cases of wrongful birth, such as when the sterilization process on a mother or father hasn't worked and a baby is born. The child then can bring a wrongful life suit (usually brought on behalf of an impaired child) saying I should not have been born." Such ideas, adds Schindler, were never considered when the insurance was written.[22]

At St. Paul, 60 percent of the claims received reflect incidents occurring in the year of treatment or the year after. Another 25 percent float in two years after treatment, 7 percent appear in the fourth year, and 8 percent appear five to ten years after treatment. The nation's biggest malpractice insurer survives these and other vicissitudes by charging higher and higher rates—up 15 to 20 percent a year in the early 1980s and up 25 to 30 percent in 1984. "It's not a matter of shafting anyone," says Nardi. "For insurance to survive, it is necessary to charge an adequate rate."[23] (It's also important to note that some studies have shown that doctors overall pay only 3.5 percent of their gross income on insurance premiums.)

Thus, St. Paul's rates typically are 5 to 10 percent higher than those of its competitors—sometimes even 20 to 30 percent higher. The rate depends on such factors as the doctor's geographic location or specialty. To qualify for St. Paul's lowest-risk category, a doctor today should open an office in Arkansas, offer himself as a general practitioner, and perform no surgery. That way, he could obtain $1 million in coverage for $1,500 a year. As a neurosurgeon practicing in Dade County, Florida, however, the doctor would pay $65,000 for the same policy (as of early 1985). Other high-risk specialists are obstetricians, heart surgeons, and anesthesiologists.

"We've been making money," says Timothy Graham, actuarial services officer at St. Paul, "but the only way we're going to continue to make money is by getting 25 percent rate increases. Our question is, can the health care marketplace keep supporting that?"[24]

That is a good question, but it touches upon far more than simply the issue of continued insurance protection, indispensable as that is in itself. There is the concomitant issue of continued service by doctors—a protection for all of society. And there is also the issue of product availability—not simply the fun and pleasure afforded by a local ice-skating rink but the life-and-death availability of drugs, including vaccines. (We will have more on vaccines in chapter 9.)

For pharmaceutical houses, the risks encompass all kinds of products. Plaster of paris, for instance, has been used for casts for what seems to be ages. And for ages, doctors have been aware that as it sets, it gives off heat. The necessary response is to wet the plaster with cool water and allow ventilation. Sometimes, though, the patient suffers a burn—and now such a patient may well sue. The charge brought against manufacturers Johnson & Johnson in such cases is that the product is defective. The company wins most of the cases, but still, it costs money to defend, and additional perceived risk can mean higher insurance costs. "All of a sudden, we're getting hit with 10 or 12 of these cases a year, and the brand is being hit with more and more legal expenses," says Roger Fine, associate general counsel for Johnson & Johnson.[25] And as George Frazza, general counsel for the firm, notes, winning is not everything: "Even if we win almost every case against us, the few verdicts we lose engender more suits and make all the other suits more expensive and more difficult to settle. There has to come a point with a particular product, even a good product, where you say, that's enough, and you get out of the market."[26]

Consider the case of Merrell Dow, for many years makers of the morning sickness drug Bendectin. Over a twenty-seven-year period, an estimated 33 million women took Bendectin to settle their stomachs, and most of them experienced no adverse effects. But then the specter of birth defects arose, and an early trickle of lawsuits became a flood by 1983. The company's insurance premiums soared to $10 million, while Bendectin claimed an annual sales volume of $12 to $13 million a year. With no room there for any profit, Merrell Dow withdrew its product. "It was a business judgment," said a company spokesman. "Economically, it just didn't make sense anymore."[27]

Another drug product that only recently became a liability target after many years of production and use is Johnson & Johnson's Ortho-Gynol spermicidal cream. After nearly forty years on the market as the nationwide leader in the field, the spermicide was blamed in 1982 for birth defects afflicting a child in Nashville, Tennessee. The mother's suit resulted in a $5.1 million award, even though, reported the *New York Times*, "most of the medical community says there is no basis for this award, since the spermicide has not been associated with the type of birth defect the little girl suffered."[28]

Although Johnson & Johnson appealed, it soon faced three more birth-defect suits blaming Ortho-Gynol, and company officials feared a great many more. For firms such as Johnson & Johnson, as for doctors, the result of litigation is higher insurance costs—50 percent higher at Johnson & Johnson in 1985 than in 1983, with 40 percent less actual coverage. By the mid-1980s, insurers willing to cover the highest possible costs suffered by a client were more difficult to find. The practice once was to spread the risks in layers, with various insurers accepting low, middle, and high ranges of monetary risk in balance with concomitant actuarial improbability. "At the top layers, the higher risk levels of, say, $250 million and above, which used to be available quite cheaply," says Johnson & Johnson's Fine, "no one wants to write the policies any more."[29]

The scale swings another way, too. The insurance seekers often have to accept a greater deductible range at bottom (or, in effect, self-insure) to find affordable insurance at all. "The deductibles are going up, and the upper limit of insurance that's available is coming down," says Robert Johnson, president of Lederle Laboratories.[30] Assuming the maker chooses not to go out of business, the result is higher product prices for the consumer.

At Lederle, in 1983 alone, the damages sought in suits assailing its whooping cough vaccine came to 200 times the firm's sales of the vaccine. "If we don't have some predictable limit on our liability costs, we will have continuing price increases," said Lederle's Johnson.[31] Statistically, the whooping cough vaccine causes brain damage in 3.2 children out of every 1 million vaccinated. Does that mean that makers of the vaccine must plan on paying millions to each of those 3.2 children for every million innoculated, *ad infinitum?*

"The court awards keep getting higher," says Johnson. "Each [victim] looks at the last award and then bootstraps onto it, saying my injury is really worse, so if they got that much, I should get more. I don't see any end in sight."[32]

New York's Dr. Ivan K. Strausz does see one "end," however—a thoroughly unpalatable one:

> Victims of clear-cut malpractice should be compensated. Unfortunately, today it is likely that even unavoidable complications will be turned into expensive lawsuits. What we now have is a perverse lottery that primarily enriches lawyers. Doctors are exploited. . . . The public purse is plundered. It is impossible to finance and deliver health care under these circumstances. Is this really the way we want to go?[33]

9

When Goods Go Bad

PAUL BRODEUR, a *New Yorker* writer, can be considered a prime example of the crusading advocates who are thoroughly enamored of the tort liability system. Brodeur subscribes without reservation to the trial lawyers' argument of tort law as a means of deterring wrongful conduct and providing just compensation for injury victims. Brodeur's book (originally articles appearing in the *New Yorker*) is scathingly entitled *Outrageous Misconduct: The Asbestos Industry on Trial*. (The authors of *this* book have to admit, though, that they're in no position to protest polemical titles.) In it, Brodeur powerfully indicts Johns-Manville (now known as Manville) and the rest of the asbestos industry in prose that reads like a brief against Manville and its competitors—which isn't surprising, since the book seems largely based on material garnered from plaintiffs' attorneys in the asbestos cases.

Admittedly, there is much in the asbestos tale to make even a skeptic of Brodeur's tract uncomfortable. According to Brodeur, asbestos manufacturers knew all along about the lethal propensities of asbestos and had covered up those hazards for about fifty years.

But the problem is not so one-sided as Brodeur's outrage indicates. Everyone now knows that asbestos can be hazardous, but just how hazardous isn't all that clear. Nor is it clear just when society, including Manville, should have known and just what should have been done about it—especially if one foregoes the number-one weapon of trial lawyers, hindsight. As Andrew Hacker, a City University of New York social scientist, points out in one of his typically thoughtful pieces (this one, a review of Brodeur's book in *Fortune*), no one questions anymore that asbestos can lead to cancer and other lethal diseases. Its fibers, lodged in the lung, can develop symptoms gradually—over twenty years or more. But, says Hacker:

Only a small minority of those who worked with asbestos in the past will be struck down by one of . . . [the] diseases [it can cause]. Brodeur accepts an estimate that 21 million living Americans have been exposed to asbestos in the work place, and he anticipates that no more than 200,000 of them will die of an "asbestos-related" cancer. Even among the workers in this group, it will not always be clear that the fibers struck the fatal blow. Most asbestos workers, the book acknowledges, were also heavy smokers.[1]

As for what Manville and its competitors knew and when, Brodeur is trenchantly accusatory. By 1939, he indicates, the literature on asbestos "would have made a stack about two feet high"—an accumulation too big for industry doctors to have overlooked, to say the least. Indeed, research funded by the industry itself was suppressed. In 1935, for example, a trade publication of the industry was induced to ignore research on asbestos, because, in the words of an attorney for Manville at the time, "Our interests are best served by having asbestosis receive the minimum of publicity."

But, as Hacker asks, what does "cover-up" really mean when the available literature, in Brodeur's own terms, "would have made a stack about two feet high"? If the doctors working for the asbestos industry knew about the damaging research (quite apart from research the industry had commissioned—and suppressed), it was accessible to others as well, right? Nor does it suffice to assert, as Brodeur does, that there were plenty of medical doctors willing to join the side of the asbestos industry. Can we accept his theory that in the 1930s, "the vast majority of the members of the medical profession chose, through apathy, to look the other way"? Could the *entire* medical profession have been co-opted by the asbestos industry—even those not in its employ, directly or indirectly? As Hacker puts it:

> As an exercise in history, *Outrageous Misconduct* shows little perspective on its period. Before 1945 long-incubating illnesses were not much on the public mind. They were certainly not on the government's mind. Concern for workers' physical well being then centered mainly on industrial accidents, which spurred workers' compensation programs. So it is a pure exercise in hindsight to assert, as Brodeur does, that we should have had "the courage and the conviction to safeguard the health of our asbestos workers back in the 1930s and 1940s." Well, yes. And we also should have been doing more about race and sex discrimination, and eliminating hunger, and helping poor kids go to college. We can all score points by applying the sensibilities of the Seventies and Eighties to the problems of the Thirties.[2]

And then Hacker makes a point that is too often overlooked: One motive of the asbestos industry to obfuscate and even hide damaging facts was and is the American litigation system itself—the system that Brodeur so unremittingly and indiscriminately praises. "Any admission of prior knowledge, let alone words of regret," writes Hacker, "would have been cited to juries as confessions of guilt."[3] Similarly, economist-lawyer Gordon Tullock recently has pointed out the destructive incentives of the fault-based liability system to encourage *both* sides to manipulate the facts—often to suppress the truth—in pursuit of litigation strategies.

As just one more example of the degree to which the litigation system *discourages* safer procedures, consider the effect of discovery proceedings whereby plaintiffs' lawyers gain access to corporate records in their attempt to substantiate allegations of wrongdoing. During the auto safety crisis of the 1960s, W.J. Ruby, one of the principal engineers at Ford, confided that because of Ford's fear of product liability suits, he was prohibited from discussing safety in writing with his fellow workers. This forced him to walk around to see them on every detail that had to be settled, which obviously had adverse effects on safety. For Brodeur, however, the uninhibited imposition of individual jury awards in the millions of dollars is the answer to injuries stemming from the manufacture and sale of dangerous items. Only the draconian threat of massive liability, in Brodeur's view, will curb corporate-induced dangers.

But litigation, as this book has tried to demonstrate, burdens not only defendants but also plaintiffs. Largely ignored in Brodeur's narrative is the lottery effect of litigation for injury victims. As John A. McKinney, Manville's chief executive, has put it: "In one recent trial in Texas, five separate juries hearing five different cases were impaneled and heard the same evidence before the same judge in the same courtroom at the same time. Their findings ranged from no liability to punitive awards." McKinney's point is one that trial lawyers—at least in private—will readily admit. At one of their recent annual meetings, personal injury lawyers, in lecturing to their peers, repeatedly referred to Kenny Rogers's gambler's lament about knowing when to hold 'em and when to fold 'em.

What about the one-half of those asbestos claimants whose suits had been tried by August 1982 and who had lost, thereby receiving nothing? Even those who succeeded in gaining out-of-court settlements against Manville, after enduring the agony of uncertainty imposed by years of delay in the disposition of their cases, were paid, on the average, settlements around $40,000. If we subtract the huge percentage taken by their lawyers, how much is left for the seriously ill victim?

Hacker points to another theme running through *this* book—the myopic cost-benefit ratio of the tort liability system, springing from its single-minded *ex post facto* focus on the wrongdoing of the party asked to pay for injury. What, after all, are the alternatives to the defendants' conduct? As Hacker puts it:

> In depicting problems with asbestos as an exercise in good vs. evil, **Outrageous Misconduct** seems oblivious to the importance of asbestos in our economy, and not only in the Thirties. Although the book devotes part of a chapter to the history of asbestos, it rather leaves you thinking that we could well do without the stuff. In fact, we still depend on it for some 2,500 products, including insulation and roofing, sewer pipes and brake linings. Nor does the book mention that Manville and other companies have been looking for substitutes for many years. Unfortunately the replacements thus far proposed seem less effective or far more costly, and some appear no less hazardous than asbestos.[3]

For Brodeur, anyone (such as Senator Gary Hart of Colorado) who suggests simpler, less accusatory compensation plans to deal with illness or injury in our society seems like a running-dog of the most pernicious features of capitalism. (Manville headquarters are in Colorado, and Brodeur traces sinister implications from relatively insignificant campaign contributions to Hart from Manville's chief executive and the Manville PAC. Would that it were all so easy—politically, socially, morally.[4]

Contrary to Brodeur's thesis, suit can often be counterproductive in both measuring and supposedly encouraging safety. This point is graphically illustrated by recent litigation in the case *Johnson v. American Cyanamid Co.*, described in an insightful article in *Regulation* magazine by University of Virginia law professor Edmund Kitch.

Keep in mind that manufacturers (and other sellers) of goods increasingly are being held liable not only for the occasional product that deviates from appropriate design—for example, metal fatigue stemming from error in the casting of the metal—but also for a whole line of products that are supposedly defective in design in the first place. Following this latter route, the courts, in a naive and clumsy manner, have wandered into the tricky engineering domain of the subtle and sometimes racking trade-offs involved in designing products.

The problem is that judges and juries—almost always with little or no engineering or scientific expertise or even background—turn out to be poor product designers. The basic problem, once again, is that they make such judgments *ex post facto*, with only the injured plaintiff in front of them. This almost inevitably has meant that courts give insufficient attention to the risks and benefits that are *not* before them. Thus, if a product has made a hundred persons safer than before but has injured the plaintiff, the court is inclined to focus on only the injury to the plaintiff. As Peter Huber, a scholarly young Washington, D.C., lawyer, has put it, the manufacturer of a product that saves *many* more lives than it puts to risk still looks like the devil incarnate in a courtroom battle against the one-in-a-million victim who is (arguably) grievously injured by the product.

Professor Kitch cites the judicial treatment of vaccines as a prime example. It's hard to imagine any modern product that produces vaster benefits to society than vaccines—benefits that clearly outweigh the occasional adverse results. And yet decisions of the courts are mindlessly and myopically threatening to cut off both existing vaccines and promising new ones.

In 1984, a Kansas jury in the *Johnson* case awarded a $10 million verdict against American Cyanamid (doing business as Lederle Laboratories) based on the proposition that the defendant should have used the Salk vaccine instead of the Sabin vaccine in polio immunization. In fact, if such a switch were to be made, polio cases in the United States would increase annually from about thirty to several thousand. As Kitch describes it, this case—and numerous cases like it—illustrates how simple-minded court decisions unwittingly threaten the public health in order to confer benefits far in excess of actual losses upon a few grievously suffering plaintiffs.

The controversy over Sabin oral polio vaccine goes back a long way and involves, as Kitch tells us, "one of the most long-standing and bitter controversies in modern medical science."[5] Originally, the polio vaccine used in the United States and elsewhere was the Salk killed-virus vaccine. Despite its use, some ten years after it had been administered on a widespread basis, thousands of polio cases still plagued the U.S. population. Thereupon, the federal Advisory Committee on Immunization Practices (ACIP), which sets standards for the administration of polio vaccines in the United States, recommended that Sabin live-virus polio vaccine be substituted for the Salk killed-virus type. The ACIP did so for several reasons, as Kitch tells us. In the first place, because the Sabin vaccine is taken orally rather than by injection, it is more easily and therefore more widely administered. Second, others in contact with the immunized party would have immunity conferred on them by the live vaccine despite not being directly vaccinated themselves. Third, a stronger and longer-lasting immunity apparently results. Except for the rare case of polio caused by the vaccine itself, the change to the Sabin vaccine eradicated polio in the United States. But, as Kitch also tells us, the struggle between adherents of the Salk and Sabin vaccines continued to rage.

Scandinavian countries, for example, continued to rely on the Salk vaccine, which doesn't seem to risk causing polio itself. In 1977, a panel from the National Academy of Sciencies recommended that the Salk vaccine be used before administration of the Sabin vaccine to protect against the Sabin while retaining its enhanced immunization. As Professor Kitch puts it:

> Whether this strategy would actually work has not been confirmed; it is, however, clear that unimmunized contacts of the recipient would also have to take Salk first if they were to be provided with additional protection. ACIP did not change its recommendation in response to the Academy's decision, although the package insert for the Sabin vaccine now advises that contacts should be informed of the opportunity to take Salk vaccine first. Sales of Salk vaccine in the United States remain small.[6]

In 1975, the Sabin oral polio vaccine was given to a child of Emil Johnson; in a short time, Emil himself became ill, but it was not clear why. In the resulting trial, Lederle disputed the contention that Emil's illness was, in fact, polio.

The plaintiff's strategy in the *Johnson* case was to discredit the Sabin vaccine, using as an expert witness a son of Jonas Salk, the creator of the Salk vaccine. According to Daryl Salk, the Sabin vaccine was too dangerous for use. His testimony was buttressed by a videotaped deposition from a Swedish immunization expert, Dr. Batenger, stating that the Sabin vaccine was considered too dangerous in Sweden and that the Salk vaccine was being used there instead.

Kitch captures the flavor of the emotional pull—and the potential danger—of tort litigation by quoting from the opening statement of plaintiff Johnson's lawyer.

> Now, another thing we contend that American Cyanamid did wrong in this case was . . . they knew, they and the government . . . really pulled the wool over everybody's eyes together. [T]hey knew that this vaccine had the following characteristics. . . . [T]hat it had a live virus in it that would be shed by the person it was given to, and that by that shedding process of the fecal material, and also by oral shedding, slobbering, drools, kissing the baby, whatever, that by that process other people would be immunized. That is to say, if Joe Smith, a member of the public who had not been immunized, went to visit his brother, Jim Smith, and they had a baby that had received . . . [the vaccine], the government and Lederle . . . knew that anyone handling that person who had received the [vaccine] . . . would also get vaccinated. And in the process, that the vaccine that was given to the baby might get stronger or more virulent and give the person polio.

> Now, admittedly, it was not something that happened very often. But it happened often enough that you're going to find that five to ten people in this country every year have been paralyzed or died as a result of it. Unknowingly and without their consent.... And the government and Lederle knew it and sacrificed those people without telling them.... [W]e contend that you assess punitive damages to set an example to that company, to say, "Hey, this is not fair. We're going to set an example, and you don't do this anymore, [we're] going to punish you."[7]

Kitch then compares the opening statement with the terms of the package insert that had been used with the Sabin vaccine at the time Emil Johnson's child was vaccinated:

> Paralytic disease following the ingestion of live poliovirus vaccines has been reported in individuals receiving the vaccine, and in some instances, in persons who were in close contact with subjects who had been given live oral poliovirus vaccine. Fortunately, such occurrences are rare, but considering the epidemiological evidence developed with respect to the total group of "vaccine related cases" it is believed by some that at least some of the cases were caused by the vaccine. The estimated risk of vaccine-induced paralytic disease occurring in vaccines or those in close contact with vaccines is extremely low. A total of approximately 30 of such cases were reported for the 8 year period covering 1963 to 1970, during which time about 147,000,000 doses of the vaccine were distributed nationally. Even though this risk is low, it should always be a source of consideration.[8]

In effect, plaintiff's lawyer was inducing a jury to overrule the government's polio vaccine policy by imposing punitive damages against a corporation that had followed government policy. But ought such a decision be made by twelve randomly selected persons, inflamed by a skilled plaintiff's lawyer? (What was it that the English legal humorist A.P. Herbert called a jury—twelve people of average ignorance?) Not only are such jurors untrained for the task of deciding national policy on polio vaccine, but their determination is dominated not by the impressive (but absent) beneficiaries of government policy but only by an isolated, if tragic, victim of that policy, standing before them. This is not to say that some way of compensating the occasional victim of government policy ought not to be sought (more on that later). Here, however, it was not only compensation being imposed on the defendant but also damages far in excess of the plaintiff's economic losses—that is, *punitive* damages as well. Punitive damages, as any first-year law student knows, are supposedly reserved for "outrageous" conduct. Clearly, the package insert in the *Johnson* case *did* seek to warn of the possibility of contracting polio from the vaccine. One can argue whether the warning might have been strengthened. (Indeed, plaintiff's lawyer had used an internal Lederle memo calling for a stronger warning in light of earlier litigation; according to the plaintiff's lawyer, the memo indicated that Lederle had engaged in intentional deception.) But one must keep in mind that a warning overstating the risk poses another sort of risk for those who are thereby deterred from using the vaccine.

If, as Kitch suggests, cases like *Johnson* actually stand for the implicit proposition that sellers should be insurers for all the adverse side effects of vaccines, then the courts have bitten off a very large bite indeed. As Kitch asks:

> Why should vaccines, one of the most successful health technologies of the century, be singled out for such a harsh rule? Why should the rule be imposed on vaccines but not, for instance, on automobiles which, exactly in the same sense as "cause" is used in the vaccine cases, "cause" death and injury on the highways? Is it socially more important to have inexpensive cars than to have inexpensive vaccines?[9]

As this book goes to press, the *Johnson* decision was reversed by a 4–3 vote of the Kansas Supreme Court, but the ominous effects of the original verdict still threaten. In the first place, the case is by no means an isolated example. Indeed, it is only one of several similar cases cited by Kitch in his article. Second, it was by no means inevitable that the decision would be reversed. If only one judge had voted differently, it would not have been. Given that appellate courts understandably presume the validity of trial court verdicts, the propensity of trial courts to award huge damages in such cases is understandably alarming to the American business community, including insurance companies. It seems even more so to the European insurance community, which plays such a large part in reinsuring American business activity. All potential defendants must have found ominous, in particular, the Kansas Supreme Court's minority opinion, which stated that since Johnson was totally incapacitated, it was "unfair to deny him any remedy whatsoever." In other words, the minority seems to say Johnson was so badly injured that he ought to have a chance to make *someone* pay.

Plaintiffs' lawyers argue that decisions like that of the trial court in the *Johnson* case "send American industry a message." Indeed they do, but it is often a very different message from the salutary one supposed by plaintiffs' lawyers. In the *Johnson* case, was the trial court's message to draft a better warning? Given the facts in the *Johnson* case, that's doubtful. And how many years of litigation would it take to find out if a new warning will fare any better? (Quite conceivably, another jury down the line, faced with an injured victim deterred from taking the vaccine by a more stringent warning, might find the new warning improper—maybe even "outrageously" so.) No, the signal sent by cases like the *Johnson* case to at least some vaccine manufacturers is simply to stop producing vaccines. When liability costs dwarf revenues, what else can one expect? Kitch cites an example: "The DPT [pertussis] vaccine is administered three times to about 3 million children a year, at a wholesale price that was until recently about a dime a dose. One tort verdict can exceed that $900,000 in annual revenue." (Kitch reports a price increase to $2.80 a dose as of June, 1985; by February, 1986, it had increased to $4.25, partly due to rising legal and insurance costs, and by May 1986, to $11.40, due to Lederle's loss of insurance coverage and the necessity to self-insure. Lederle says of the new price, $8.00 will be to cover its potential liability.) Predicting accurately the outcome of highly unpredictable litigation, says Kitch, "will often move production away from technologically superior and well financed firms which have the most to lose [from litigation]."[10] The result is that only a single producer remains in the United States for vaccines for such maladies as measles, mumps, rubella, polio, and rabies. What happens, then, when such a manufacturer runs into difficulty? In the fall of 1984, when one producer withdrew a batch of its DPT vaccine as substandard, the Advisory Committee on Immunization Practices (ACIP) was forced to recommend reduced and rationed use of the vaccine.

Who will want to be in a business so dependent on what Kitch calls a "hostile and unpredictable legal regime"?[11] The incentives to innovate are already low in the vaccine industry because, unlike most pharmaceuticals, the product is taken only once or at most a few times. The lack of incentive already inclines a manufacturer to market other products that call for continuing (and therefore more profitable) ingestion. And how many years will it take to determine whether and to what extent a new vaccine will have adverse side effects? If the courts are going to hammer the manufacturer for perhaps only arguable side effects, as Kitch puts it, such liability "would wipe out any possible profit from even a fabulously successful (in a medical sense) vaccine."[12] Won't the development and manufacture of a vaccine for AIDS or herpes be hindered in such an environment? If the personal injury bar boasts of the beneficiaries of product liability law, who represents the would-be beneficiaries of a technology foregone under the threat of product liability law?

10

Reforming Reforms

IS there a solution to this mess? For the insurance industry and its institutional clients—businesses, health care providers, local and state governments, and so on—the answer is *tort reform*, by which they mean statutes that would curtail what they perceive as the excesses of the tort system. Specifically, they propose:

1. Limiting pain-and-suffering awards to, say, $100,000 or $250,000 or $500,000.
2. Eliminating or severely curbing the occasions when punitive damages can be awarded.
3. Limiting plaintiffs' lawyers' contingent fees to curb the incentives for lawyers to press litigation—for example, 40 percent of the first $50,000, with the share dwindling by steps to only 10 percent of any recovery over $200,000.
4. Deducting from amounts payable by the defendant any other insurance already payable to the plaintiff from, say, health or disability insurance.
5. Eliminating or restricting the application of strict liability under which a seller can be held liable for a defective product even though he was not in any way negligent. (Actually, strict liability may not be a key cause of the insurance miseries plaguing those currently being sued, a point indicated by the fact that the "strict" concept applies only to products, not to services, such as health care—yet health care providers are facing the same problems of arguably unmanageable liability as are sellers of products.)
6. Abolishing or altering the doctrine of "joint and several liability," under which a defendant (such as a park district) that is only 1 or 2 percent negligent can be held liable for almost the entire award of millions of

dollars if another party that is overwhelmingly more at fault in causing the accident (say, a manufacturer of playground equipment) is either insolvent or grossly underinsured. Under this reform, a defendant's share of any award would be limited to a share of blame; thus, the defendant who was found to be 25 percent at fault would be liable, at most, for 25 percent of any damage award.

Some such reforms have been enacted in several states, including California, Missouri, and Indiana, and they are under consideration everywhere else. Even the Reagan administration has proposed such reforms, despite a conservative federal administration's natural reluctance to invade a domain traditionally controlled by states' rights.[1]

To support such proposals, doctors and business executives have been staging massive and well-publicized marches in Washington, D.C., and in state capitals all over the country. Said Congressman Thomas Luken (D.-Ohio) at one such rally, "Probably no recent issue has snowballed so quickly."[2]

A "solution" to the problems created by current tort law that merely further restricts compensation for claims is a questionable solution indeed. As one might imagine, too, the response of the trial bar to such proposals has been outrage. Says Robert Habush, president of the Association of Trial Lawyers of America, "In my 25 years in law, this is as serious a threat to the civil justice system as I have ever seen. People have decided there is going to be a hanging, and it is just a question of what tree and what rope."[3] The trial bar has skillfully enlisted the support of many consumer groups, including Ralph Nader's organizations, in opposing such reforms. Some thirty consumer groups have formed a new association called the Coalition for Consumer Justice to oppose the tort reforms being proposed by the insurance industry and its corporate insureds. Its president, Naderite Joan Claybrook, says that its purpose is to "counteract a nationwide lobbying campaign by the insurance industry to limit the legal rights of innocent consumers and victims."[4] The Coalition charges that a "massive assault" has been launched, seeking to dismantle the civil justice system. Likewise, J. Robert Hunter, an insurance industry gadfly and president of the Nader-founded and -funded National Insurance Consumer Organization, noted recently at an Illinois legislative hearing: "If the tobacco industry came in here and said "We're having a little trouble with our profit. Would you mind putting a cap on civil rights?' You'd toss them out of here."[5] Said Jay Angoff, another official of the National Insurance Consumer Organization, in testimony before a U.S. Senate committee: "Our organization thinks that the reason for the shortage of insurance is that the insurance companies have been mismanaged in the past. They are not losing money; they are just doing less well."[6] Angoff cited data collected by the General Accounting Office of the U.S. Congress showing that liability insurers generally experience fluctuations in income but that in the long run, they are no less profitable than other U.S. industries taken as a whole.

According to Angoff, the reason for the fluctuations and the current insurance malaise is that insurance companies need to attract premium income during times of high inflation in order to reap investment income, which leads them to write high-risk policies at low rates in order to compete with other insurers also seeking premium—and therefore investment—income. But, testified Angoff, when inflation is lower, as it became in the mid-1980s, insurers that are unable to find high-interest investments suddenly shunned their risky policies. As Robert Hunter has lectured the insurance industry: "At the top of the cycle you write [policies for] everybody, no matter how bad, and at the bottom you cancel everybody, no matter how good. It's a manic-depressive cycle."[7]

In congressional testimony, Ralph Nader himself charged that the insurance industry has gone "berserk," first slashing premiums drastically in the late 1970s and early 1980s to procure cash flow to invest, and then drastically increasing rates after the industry hit bottom in 1984. Not satisfied with fleecing thousands of businesses, such as day-care centers, charged Nader, the insurance industry now wants to take away basic rights of citizens. In this respect, Nader was echoing the remarks of Gerry Spence, a legendary Wyoming personal injury lawyer who has remarked: "What the insurance companies have done is to reverse the business so that the public at large insures the insurance companies."

Nader was particularly incensed at Lloyds of London, accusing the London market of trying to force the United States into reducing accident victim rights under American common law. According to Nader (never short of rhetoric), the London market is acting like "King Lloyd," reviving memories of that earlier British tyrant, King George.

The trial lawyers and their allies in the consumer movement insist that insurance companies are using the shortage of insurance coverage—which they created—to conspire to charge exorbitant premiums and/or even to withdraw from writing coverages in order to curtail the rights of injured parties.

As usual, Nader has a point—but this time only part of one. It *is* unfair, as the trial lawyers and their allies in the consumer groups point out, to reform the tort system—a system under which, as we've seen, it is very tough for an injured person, especially a seriously injured person, to be paid—by making it even tougher to get paid or more likely to be paid a lot less when one is paid. As the trial lawyers and their consumer allies have pointed out, there *is* a lot of wrongdoing out there. One cannot ignore the asbestos tale told by Paul Brodeur nor the tragic aftermath of A.H. Robins's Dalkon Shield intrauterine device—in the form of claims for punctured and destroyed uteruses, pelvic infections, spontaneous abortions, damaged infants, and the like.

At a 1986 hearing on hospital safety held by New York City Council President Andrew J. Stein, David G. Starks, deputy director for health care, standards, and surveillance in the New York State Health Department, testified that the following incidents had occurred during the previous year at hospitals in the city: At the Baptist Medical Center in Brooklyn, the mouth and nostrils of one patient became infested with maggots because of substandard medical and nursing care. Another patient at the same hospital died during surgery because of an inadequate diagnosis. At the Harlem Hospital Center, a surgeon's error in repairing a knee led to the necessity of amputating the patient's leg. At the Kings County Hospital Center, an AIDS patient died after his dialysis treatment was curtailed.

Unquestionably, the availability of civil remedies to redeem such wrongs remains very vital, from the point of view of both basic justice and basic economics. Some doctors will admit in private that the threat of malpractice litigation has led to greater care and concern for patients (in a profession sometimes notorious for its arrogance and indifference to individual patients).

As to product liability, Robert H. Malott, chairman of FMC Corporation and head of the Business Roundtable's task force on product liability, states that "the crisis in liability insurance has made risk management a main concern for top corporate decision-makers."[8] As an example, *Fortune* magazine cites the instance several years ago when manufacturers were faced with a spate of tort claims over multipiece truck wheel rims, which can explode once huge, high-pressure tires are mounted on them. In response, top management turned to Failure Analysis Associates of Palo Alto, California, a large engineering firm that has an extensive data base on accident severity and frequency. A Failure Analysis statistical engineering study showed that the multipiece rims have accident rates no higher than those of single-piece rims and that the actual culprit was the procedure mechanics were using to inflate and mount the tires. As a result, industrywide training standards were instituted that, in turn, reduced injury rates by 80 percent.[9]

In answer to trial lawyers and consumer advocates, however, any conspiracy theory for explaining the constricted insurance market is, like all conspiracy theories, hard to substantiate. The insurance industry consists of more than 900 companies, all competing for business. If there is so much money to be made in writing insurance, why are so many companies withdrawing from so many lines of coverage? And why, for example, are the mutual companies owned by doctors themselves joining in "gouging" their own members? At the same Illinois hearing at which J. Robert Hunter testified, Bob Miller, government relations director for Allstate, a leading casualty insurer, challenged Hunter's premise of an industrywide cartel. "Why would we collude to lose money instead of [to] make money?" he asked.[10] According to Lyndon Olson, chairman of the Texas Board of Insurance, the state's regulatory body: "These folks [insurance executives] are too greedy to collude."

Consumer advocates, however, return to the attack with data purporting to deny any litigation explosion justifying increased liability insurance rates. Recently, the National Center for State Courts, a research organization located in Williamsburg, Virginia, released figures indicating that no litigation explosion exists—or at least if there ever was one it ended in 1981. As to tort suits, the study purports to show that any increase in filings since 1978 has only followed the rise in population. But the U.S. Justice Department strongly disagrees. According to Robert Willmore of the department's civil division:

> There is no question but that we have a serious litigation problem in certain areas, including medical malpractice, product liability, and municipal liability. The center's statistics on state courts group all torts together and say there's no problem. But if you look at the Federal court statistics, which separate out the different categories of torts, you can see that the number of automobile accident cases is going way down, while the number of product liability cases is going way up.[11]

Marc Galanter, a leading expert on litigation statistics, sides with the National Center. "There hasn't been any exponential increase in the use of the courts," he says. "Some areas, such a product liability, have unquestionably been growth areas for litigation, while other areas, such as class actions, are declining."[12] In his view, even the increase in product liability claims is mostly attributable to asbestos cases. On the subject of non-auto cases, a General Accounting Office (GAO) study purports to show that although medical malpractice and general liability premiums account for less than 10 percent of the insurance industry's premiums, they account for

24 percent of its underwriting lawsuits. The GAO contends that even there the industry could have broken even by a 20 percent raise in medical malpractice premiums and a 30 percent increase for general liability. The Justice Department's Mr. Willmore retorts by saying, "That's not how insurance works. The industry can't just cover past losses. It has to predict what's going to happen in the future. And what they are facing is a deteriorating tort system."[13]

In such a view, it is not so much a question of how much insurance companies have collected in the past, as how much they will need in the future. Given all the uncertainty generated by the tort system, those faced with covering future losses make a plausible case of how hard it is to predict what future claims will cost. In short, our highly volatile tort system seems finally to be catching up with—and arguably even surpassing—the parts of our economy exposed to liability for personal injury.

Quite apart from how much liability insurance should cost, the present tort system, which is premised on findings of fault and which pays for noneconomic loss, is a wildly fortuitous, expensive, and dilatory way of not only 1) deterring unsafe conduct, but also 2) compensating injury victims.

Even if the statements of the insurance industry and its corporate insureds are questionable as a basis for instituting reform—and granting that the least appealing way to reform the tort system is to make it even harder for the seriously injured to be paid—the present system seems intolerable. Thus, even if liability insurance rates were not rising, and even if professionals and corporate insureds were finding it easy to buy liability insurance, the tort liability system would still be in need of drastic change—especially from the point of view of those who are injured. But not only from their perspective; also to correct the profligate misuse of dollars in litigation costs that all consumers are paying, even assuming that the price of insurance is readily affordable. That is why it is so tragic to see consumer groups feverishly allying with trial lawyers in defense of this cruel, corrupt, and capricious system. If consumer activists seem to be right in opposing changes that simply make it tougher for the injured to be paid, they also seem to be wrong in clinging to the system that already makes it much too tough to be paid. Note, in this regard, that trial lawyers are hoist by their own petard. They have to concede that it's very hard—especially for the severely injured—to get payment under tort liability; how else can they justify charging a third or more to help get it?

For the answer to the insurance liability mess, we turn first, in the next chapter, to the subject of auto accidents.

11

No Fault, No Fee

IF the liability crisis as a whole seems to defy solution, there is one substantial chunk of it that need not: auto accident cases. Happily for many of us, too, Tom Dunkel, writing in the *New Jersey Monthly*, has managed to breathe recognizable life into this often moribund, always arcane domain of certain lawyers and insurers. Rather than instigate the usual glaze in the eyes accompanying such discussion, Dunkel has rendered the controversy over auto insurance in demystifying terms:

> Since insurance ranks right up there with photosynthesis on the ho-hum scale, the only way to muddle through this controversy is to inject a little drama into it. Don't think of auto insurance as auto insurance. Think of it as a prize fight. A real knock-down, drag-out marathon slugfest. In one corner is "Killer" Tort, the slow-footed, hard-punching veteran who represents the "you-smashed-into-my-car-and-now-I'm-going-to-sue-your-pants-off" old school of claims settlement. His opponent is "Kid" No-Fault, a quick-moving young challenger who has never quite lived up to his potential. The "Kid" takes the gentlemanly approach to all accidents: Why get uptight about who's at fault? Let's just get the bills paid and the cars on the road.
>
> Like any good fight this one has a lot riding on the outcome, namely the $2.5 billion annually spent on car insurance in [New Jersey]. Given the stakes it's no wonder the pugs are being managed by a couple of hard-bitten pros. "Killer" Tort has New Jersey's legal establishment behind him, while "Kid" No-Fault is in the good hands of the insurance industry.
>
> What makes this boxing match unique is that it's the spectators, not the fighters, who take the pounding. The Killer and the Kid trade jabs, but the consumer is the one getting bruised and bloodied. . . .
>
> [T]he good news from ringside is everybody agrees that, although auto rates are destined to be high, they don't have to be *that* high. The problem is that nobody agrees on how to ease the financial burden on motorists. Last

February Joseph Tomeo, a 44-year-old millwright from Pennsville, organized a consumer group called New Jersey AIR (Automobile Insurance Reform) partly to find out why, as a married man with a perfect driving record, he is paying $1400 a year to insure two automobiles.

"When you talk to a lawyer, he blames it on the insurance agent," says Tomeo, who uses his vacation days to lobby in Trenton. "When you talk to an insurance agent, he blames it on the lawyers. You talk to a legislator, he's either a lawyer or an insurance agent."[1]

The case for no-fault insurance was and remains simple and compelling: the traditional, tort-law process of fault-finding gobbles up time and money that could be spent compensating people who need help. Under a pure tort system, as discussed earlier for all kinds of accidents, if a driver suffers injuries from a car accident, he is not automatically entitled to compensation from his own insurance company. Before he can collect, he must demonstrate to a jury that *another* driver was responsible for the accident. If the victim wins, the wrongdoer (or, actually, the wrongdoer's insurance company) must pay him not only for his out-of-pocket expenses—medical costs and lost wages—but also for the "pain and suffering" that results from the injury. If he loses, he gets nothing.

In contrast, under no-fault, an accident victim does not need to prove that anyone was at fault before he gets his money, and payment is limited to his economic loss. Thus, at a stroke, the two variables lawyers spend so much time and money arguing over—who is at fault and what pain is worth—are eliminated. A no-fault policy insures a motorist for his actual losses under any circumstance that might injure him. The harm might come from another driver; but it might come from the victim's own regrettable carelessness, a situation the tort system cannot address. Consider a collision with a stationary object. If you crash into a tree, you'll have a hard time convincing a jury that it ran out into the middle of the road. (Trees in any case tend to be insolvent.) Or consider a two-car collision that injures the driver who caused the accident. Under the tort system, if you're at fault, you can't collect.

And what about the broad, gray area in which most traffic accidents occur—cases in which both drivers are at fault? Maybe one fellow was speeding because he was a little anxious about being late for an important business meeting. Maybe the other driver was looking out the window at an attractive woman who was crossing the street. The tort system's unhappy solution is to have the two men slug it out in court over who was more guilty. Under no-fault, the question is irrelevant.

The difference no-fault can make in the lives of auto accident victims was dramatically illustrated by two cases cited in a 1984 issue of *Consumer Reports*.[2] In Illinois, which operates under the tort system, 25-year-old Robert Demichelis was returning home from a basketball game at Northern Illinois University when he dozed off at the wheel. His Datsun 200SX bounced off a guard rail and smashed into a concrete divider in the middle of the interstate. Demichelis's head struck the windshield, and he suffered brain damage. His ability to reason and make judgments was sufficiently impaired that he was unable to hold a job. Health insurance helped cover some of his medical bills, but his family ended up paying for his rehabilitation treatments. At the time the *Consumer Reports* article appeared, Demichelis's family had paid out $15,000. Because they had no one to sue, there was no auto insurance money to cover the cost.

The second case took place in Michigan, which has the most comprehensive no-fault law in the country. Thirteen-year-old Faith Ann Glynn was riding her bicycle when a car struck her from behind. Glynn, like Demichelis, suffered brain damage. In addition to having two brain operations, she lived in nursing and rehabilitation centers for two years. But in Glynn's case, the automobile insurance company that covered the entire family picked up all her medical expenses. It didn't matter that Glynn hadn't been driving a car; the coverage extended to auto accidents that occurred when a member of the family was walking or riding a bicycle.

Of course, if Faith Glynn had been injured in a state operating under the tort system, she would have been able to sue the driver. But tort awards are limited by the extent of the wrongdoer's liability coverage, for which states generally set a minimum of only $10,000 or $20,000. (Glynn's medical bills and rehabilitation treatment, all paid by her family's auto insurance, came to more than $180,000.) Although it's true that most people take out insurance in excess of the minimum, there's no guarantee that the fellow who crashes into you will—and under a tort system, it's the other guy's coverage that determines how much you collect. No-fault, by contrast, removes this anxiety, since what matters is not anybody else's coverage but your own. And that coverage can be more generous because of money saved by avoiding the courtroom. (Thanks in substantial measure to lawyers' fees, only 44 cents of every dollar paid into liability insurance pools ever makes it into the pockets of accident victims.) This is not to say that no-fault is prone to making extravagant awards. No, no-fault does not pay for "pain and suffering." Further, it also caps the possible recovery for lost wages and can subtract compensation made to the victim under other insurance programs. Finally, payments are made as medical and other bills fall due, rather than later from those purely speculative lump sums that, in amount and uncertainty, make trial awards resemble a grotesque sweepstakes.

If no-fault's virtues are so obvious, why isn't the idea spreading—and why are some states actually turning against it? We can begin to answer this question by looking at the halfhearted way in which most no-fault legislation has been drafted. Most states have chosen to water down the no-fault principle in one of two ways.

The first is to set thresholds that must be reached—most commonly, medical expenses in excess of a certain dollar amount before an injury victim may bring legal action. The states that have adopted this form of no-fault—sixteen of the twenty-four that have no-fault—are called "no-lawsuit" states. This is a serious misnomer. Lawsuits still are routine in most of these states. The dollar thresholds for medical expenses above which tort claims can still be pressed range from as low as $200 (New Jersey) to as high as $4,500 (Minnesota). Obviously, it doesn't take much of an injury to come away from the doctor with a $200 bill. And even when the dollar threshold is high, doctors with an eye on the "pain-and-suffering" jackpot, which, as we've seen, typically pays off at three to five times the amount of real economic loss, may be tempted to pad costs. (One doctor charged with cost-padding was the proud owner of a yacht called "Whiplash.")

A better way to set thresholds is through categories of harm—for example, permanent disability, serious disfigurement, or the loss of a limb. Such "verbal" thresholds tend to be more restrictive than monetary thresholds, with the result that the no-lawsuit states with verbal thresholds—Michigan, New York, and Florida—end up having far fewer lawsuits.

The second method of watering down no-fault is to place no restrictions at all on the right to sue and merely to require that insurers sell—and, in some case, that drivers buy—no-fault insurance. Eight of the twenty-four no-fault states have adopted this form of no-fault, including Texas, Maryland, and Oregon. In these "add-on" states, no-fault is watered down even more than it is in the no-lawsuit states, since the courts remain open to all accident victims.

In both the no-lawsuit and the add-on states, there is one further problem: insurance companies are required to offer only a limited amount of no-fault coverage—sometimes as little as a few thousand dollars. This leaves anyone with a serious injury no choice but to resort to the courtroom. But consider Michigan, which enacted no-fault in 1975. Michigan is a no-lawsuit state with a tough verbal threshold: only those accident victims who can show that they have suffered "serious impairment of a bodily function" or "permanent serious disfigurement" have access to the courtroom. (Families of those whose injuries result in death may also sue.) By saving on court battles, Michigan is able to offer unlimited no-fault medical benefits; there is no cap on what victims like Faith Ann Glynn can collect from their insurer. At the same time, Michigan enjoys relatively low auto insurance premiums; in 1985, the U.S. Department of Transportation found that they were 17 percent less than they would have been had no-fault not been enacted.

The stunningly favorable contrast of the relatively low premium cost of high levels of payments under no-fault compared to the relatively high premium cost of low levels of payments under traditional coverage is perhaps best illustrated by New York State. No-fault benefits there are available for medical expenses and wage loss up to a combined total of $50,000. Lawsuits based on fault are allowed when the victim is disabled for ninety days or when the victim dies or suffers other serious injury. For tort purposes required tort insurance minimums are only $10,000 per person and $20,000 per accident. The 1983 New York average annual premium for no-fault insurance for $46, whereas the average premium for tort injury liability coverage was $118. In other words, no-fault premiums cost much less than half the tort liability premiums, but the no-fault coverage pays automatically for benefits up to $50,000 per injured person in case of accident, whereas the liability coverage often pays far less in benefits, and only upon proof of fault. A similar situation exists in other no-fault states.

Why haven't no-fault laws been enacted everywhere, and why have there often been crippling compromises when they have been enacted? Blame a small group of self-interested professionals who see a serious threat to their livelihood in the passage of tougher no-fault laws. Most of the nation's trial lawyers earn their bread and butter through tort law; fees in auto accident cases alone top $1 billion annually. Obviously, these fees are threatened by no-fault. Whereas upwards of 80 percent of all tort cases—and certainly all high-stakes tort cases—require the services of a lawyer, only 15 percent of all no-fault claims do. Small wonder, then, that the lawyers have done everything they can to strangle no-fault in the crib.

The Association of Trial Lawyers of America (ATLA) annually doles out huge sums in political contributions, routinely focusing on issues related to tort law, including no-fault. The ATLA can take much of the credit for the defeat of a bill before Congress in the late 1970s that would have required states to adopt no-fault laws with minimum coverage of $100,000 for medical expenses and $24,000 for rehabilitation. Equally important have been similar groups operating at the grass-roots level—such as Attorneys Devoted to Ohio People Totally (ADOPT), which targeted state legislators who favored no-fault.

Lawyers have an additional advantage in manipulating the political system because they tend to be active in political campaigns. Unlike steelworkers, for example, trial lawyers are able to organize their time schedules by obtaining continuances past election day; indeed, after early November in election years, trial calendars are frequently jammed, and most courthouses look like Grand Central Station. Consider, also, the experience of one 1972 Democratic candidate for governor in a major northeastern industrial state. "In community after community," said one key aide, "we checked and found that plaintiffs' lawyers were campaign or finance chairmen. . . . They would not have tolerated a pro-no-fault stand. Our organization might well have fallen apart." Lawyers are also vastly overrepresented in state legislatures across the country. The brotherhood of the bar is obviously felt when it comes time for a roll call.

Of course, the trial lawyers insist that more is at stake than their own self-interest. "We don't give a damn what the cynics say," says one former ATLA president. "We want our views debated not on who represents them but on who they affect, and that's our clients, the consumers." The argument runs something like this:

1. The great common-law tradition guarantees victims their day in court.
2. By taking cases on a contingency-fee basis, whereby an attorney is paid nothing up front but rather works for a percentage of any trial awards, plaintiffs' lawyers assure that worthy claims will be prosecuted.
3. "Pain and suffering" constitute an important and real part of loss and should be accounted for in determining appropriate compensation.
4. By punishing drivers who do things we don't want them to do, the tort system deters socially detrimental behavior.
5. Contrary to supporters' assertions, no-fault actually increases auto insurance premiums.

Let's set aside points 1 and 5 for the moment. The problem with point 2 is that contingency fees typically swallow up a third of any jury award; some lawyers go so far as to charge 50 percent. Even assuming that this incentive system is fair, it does nothing to help those whose injuries came about because of their own fault (the fellow who runs into a tree or into another driver) or those who suffer in an accident for which fault is not easy to assign (the fellow late for an appointment who runs into the fellow daydreaming about the woman). Indeed, the tort system makes the latter case worse by forcing each party to prove that the other was guilty, even though, as we've seen, this conflict, by definition, is one about which reasonable men might differ.

As for point 3, the "pain and suffering" endured by the victim of any accident is, at best, difficult to translate into a dollar figure; indeed, the worse the suffering, the more sadly inadequate monetary compensation of any kind seems. And what about the "pain and suffering" endured by accident victims, like Illinois basketball fan Robert Demichelis, who can't blame their fate on someone else? Should their economic needs go unmet while we grope to meet the less tangible needs of others? If we are going to spend money on suffering people, shouldn't we put a priority on problems we *can* solve, such as unpaid medical bills?

Moving on to point 4, the deterrent effect of the tort system is undermined by the fact that almost all court awards are covered by a wrongdoer's insurance, with the result that a negligent driver will feel the brunt of his sins only marginally, in the form of higher insurance premiums. It is not surprising that comparisons of fault and no-fault jurisdictions show no statistically significant difference in the number of accidents. In the case of the criminally reckless driver, the proper solution is vigorous enforcement of criminal laws. If a drunk or excessively careless driver poses a serious menace to society, he ought to lose his driver's licence or even go to jail.

The arguments that carry the most weight with the public, legislators, and state judges are those based on the "right to sue" and the alleged higher cost of no-fault. Local courts in Washington, D.C., and Florida have declared threshold requirements unconstitutional on the grounds they discriminate against some claimants' opportunities to collect damages for "pain and suffering." (The issue is now moot in the District of Columbia, where the city council recently gutted its no-fault statute.) Although several consumer groups—including Consumers Union, the nation's largest—have come out squarely behind the expansion of no-fault, other consumer advocates—most notably, Ralph Nader—have avoided the issue, most likely because it conflicts with the notion that the right to a day in court is fundamental for keeping misbehavior in check. But what seriously injured accident victim wants a lottery ticket? And in the case of the lone driver, whose limbs are as much at risk as those of whomever he may hit, do we need tort liability to keep him conscious of safety? (In this connection, we must note that Naderite J. Robert Hunter, president of the National Insurance Consumer Organization, parts company with his patron in supporting no-fault insurance.)

In addition, there's a precedent for denying court access to potential tort claimants, so long as they are granted other benefits in return—workers' compensation. Workers' compensation laws deprive employees of the right to sue employers for injuries occurring at the workplace but do guarantee victims basic, if not particularly extravagant, compensation regardless of questions of fault. All fifty states have long had such statutes, and imperfect though they may be, nobody is suggesting a return to fault-based law in that area.

As for the cost problems, it is true that car owners in some no-fault states have complained about substantial increases in their insurance bills. This has been the primary reason for the repeal of no-fault laws in Nevada, Pennsylvania, and the District of Columbia. But inflated prices are only the logical result of introducing no-fault without correspondingly restricting the right to sue. No-fault proponents have never pretended that no-fault could save money unless access to courts was severely restricted. In fact, in those states with highly restrictive verbal thresholds—those that most closely approximate a pure no-fault system—insurance rates, on average, have increased only slightly more than they have in traditional tort jurisdictions. And those increases have been due more to increases in the tort liability portion of the premium than to the no-fault part. What appears to happen is that no-fault benefits are used to "pad" the tort claim to make the latter worth more—in both illegitimate claims (see chapter 6) and legitimate ones. A claimant who is assured of payment of medical expenses and wage loss is also in a position to hold out for a higher amount from his tort claim, causing an increase in premiums. (Thus, Pennsylvania, in repealing its requirement that motorists carry high limits of no-fault insurance and in retaining the requirement that they carry low limits of fault-based coverage, got it exactly wrong.)

In spite of all the compromises, it's worth noting that even watered-down no-fault laws can claim significant success on several fronts. According to the Department of Transportation, no-fault compensates more people (roughly twice as many) with greater benefits (79 percent more) in quicker payments (almost all no-fault payments, as opposed to only half of all tort awards, are made during the first year following injury). No-fault has also benefited taxpayers; although no-fault hasn't reduced lawsuits as much as it should, thousands of accident-related small claims have been kept out of court, representing millions of dollars saved. (As of 1983, the average jury tort case cost taxpayers $8,300.) To cite just one example, during the four years before no-fault was enacted in Massachusetts in 1971, the average annual number of automobile tort cases was nearly 32,000; during the four years that followed no-fault enactment, the average dropped to 12,000 cases per year.[3]

But even if the political realities blunt the hope of enacting sweeping no-fault auto insurance all at once, with all its broad social benefits, it would seem only fair to allow motorists the *choice* of no-fault protection. There's an opportunity here to put the market to work, to allow an end-run around the opponents' objections by means of the powerful (and once again popular) creed of free enterprise.

As things now stand, the consumer is allowed no discretion in deciding the type of auto insurance he will have; his state government decides it for him. If you live in a fault-oriented state, you must buy a certain amount of liability insurance, but you have no opportunity to opt for no-fault coverage, even if you are willing to eschew court access privileges. In the so-called no-fault states, you must purchase some of each, again without provisions for channel-switching. There's a reason why allowing such choice wouldn't work under existing arrangements. There's also a way around the obstacle.

Unlike a choice between, say, automatic and manual transmission, auto insurance is interactive in that, under present systems, one consumer's insurance selection affects another's after the fact of an accident. If one driver negligently causes serious injury to another, the victim's possibilities for a courtroom recovery will likely depend on how large a liability insurance policy the person at fault holds. This is why most states require that all drivers have some minimum coverage. This sort of interaction would seem inevitably to cripple any plan permitting a basic choice on types of insurance. If two drivers with no-fault policies collided, there would be no problem; each would collect from his own insurer. Likewise, if each carried only third-party insurance, no difficulties would arise; the two could fight it out in court, as presumably desired. But what if a no-fault motorist ran into one holding liability insurance? Here we find the stumbling block. As a condition of his policy, Mr. No-Fault would have forsaken his right to sue, regardless of the other driver's negligence. Mr. Fault, however, would still be counting on a fault-based claim against the other motorist for his compensation. If the law allows liability insureds to bring legal action, as would surely be demanded, the no-fault holder would have to insure both against his own injuries and against any injuries of Mr. Fault, and those like him, for which he might be liable. What would the result be? No-fault coverage would end up far more expensive than third-party coverage and, despite other advantages, the built-in cost disincentive would undoubtedly dissuade motorists from making the switch. This is, in essence, the spurious "reform" of a recent amendment to the District of Columbia's no-fault statute.

But a choice scheme could become feasible with the creation of a connector with which to bridge the gap that occurs when a car with fault coverage and one with no-fault coverage collide. That mechanism is already in place. Insurance companies routinely—indeed, often are required to—offer policies to protect against accidents with uninsured motorists (UM) and against damage done by hit-and-run vehicles, coverage that compensates the holders to the same extent they would have been compensated had the faulty uninsured motorist been insured—pain, suffering, and all. UM insurance could easily be extended to treat no-fault insureds as, in effect, uninsured motorists so as to allow recovery by Mr. Fault if he were to be hit by a no-fault driver. By the same token, Mr. No-Fault, completely covered for his medical expenses and wage losses, could neither sue nor be sued on the basis of fault. Even though Mr. Fault's UM coverage costs would rise as a result of the larger class of "uninsured" drivers, his liability premiums would decrease correspondingly, in that none of the no-fault policy holders would be able to bring suit against him. The scheme would avoid pricing problems by insulating the costs of fault and no-fault policies from each other; no longer would the no-fault motorist find himself subsidizing his litigation-loving brothers. By the same token, no longer would anyone be forced to relinquish involuntarily the cherished right to be paid on a fault basis, as now happens in no-lawsuit jurisdictions.[4]

The real advantage of such a framework is that it would allow a political choice to be made in the marketplace. The driving public's collective choice would emerge from a referendum of sorts, a tally not so easily refuted by the losing side. As we have seen, in states that now require both no-fault and third-party auto insurance, the no-fault provides far more in potential benefits for the premium dollar. If past experience is any guide, we may expect a classic showing of the old voting-with-their-pocketbooks phenomenon—and a massive switch to no-fault. The trial lawyers would be hard-pressed to deny the significance of such a shift, and the collapse of their consumerist justification might mark the breach through which pure no-fault statutes could move, perhaps in the form of federal legislation. Even if both types of coverage maintain many adherents, that's acceptable too—it's no more than a matter of allowing the consumer to choose, of letting the market work.

The adoption of a choice model would itself require legislative approval; that task, however, might be lightened by the abandonment of any element of compulsion. A good idea—and a solution to auto insurance palatable enough for even cautious lawmakers to act on.

12

Neo-No-Fault

DESPITE trial lawyers' valid point that, intuitively, the tort system is sensible in that it makes a wrongdoer pay an innocent victim of his wrongdoing, the problem is that accidents happen under very complex circumstances. They happen in the split-second agony of an automobile collision or during the organized chaos of surgery. They happen when a toaster explodes or when an industrial machine malfunctions. The interconnection between a malfunctioning machine or improper procedure and the individual who is hurt can be very difficult to unravel. Even automobile accidents have proven too difficult for the law to disentangle the thread of who was at fault, as movements to no-fault insurance demonstrate (chapter 11). But when one moves from simple automobile accidents to an injury from a product, such as when a toaster explodes, one needs engineering testimony of the most arcane kind to unravel whether or not even such a relatively simple consumer machine was misused by the owner or had a defect in its myriad electronic or other complex parts. And meters are ticking all the while that lawyers and engineers are trying desperately to understand each other. This raises another problem. Engineers don't always understand much law. Indeed, some don't understand much English. Without being overly harsh, anybody who thinks in *ergs* is in trouble convincing anybody else of what he is talking about. Articulate engineers, then, can be very hard to come by. As lawyers can attest from hours spent readying engineers to testify in court, trying to get them to say what they're saying in terms understandable to jurors is *very* expensive work: because all the while a lawyer is huddling with an engineer their meters are ticking merrily away.

When one moves to medical malpractice, the complexity of the accidental event becomes truly awesome. Most machines are complicated, but the "machines" we humans walk around in almost defy description. There are, for example, some 16 billion neurons in the cortex of the human brain. If one sat down to design a machine of that complexity, one would need an Empire State Building to house it, a Niagara Falls flowing over it to handle all the friction. And yet we humans—male and female—are housed in machines of between, say, 100 and 300 pounds, in which we move around for eighty years or so with relatively little friction and normally not much need for repairs. (It's almost enough to make you religious.) But when something does go wrong and health care professionals have to repair our machines—and then something *further* goes wrong—trying to find out whether the doctor or the "machine" itself was at fault entails awesomely complicated questions. Here, too, "cultural" problems present themselves. If engineers sometimes don't understand much English, the same is true of doctors. To some, it might appear they go to medical school never to speak English again. They learn a bastardized form of Greek, of which they are ostentatiously proud. It is only under the most intense pressure that they can be induced to return to the language of their childhood, to which the lawyer must coax them back for the jury's edification—again with the expensive meters ticking all around.

The result is that finding fault, even if it intuitively makes sense, is often an extremely expensive and cumbersome business in both simple and complex product liability or medical malpractice cases.

It is very significant that no other form of insurance pays on the basis of fault. When you die, your life insurance company cannot refuse payment on the grounds that you smoked too much or ate too many fatty foods. When a woman becomes pregnant, her health insurer doesn't make any inquiries about whose "fault" it was. And when your house burns down, your fire insurance company cannot resist payment on the grounds you were smoking in bed or left some oily rags under the cellar stairs. In each of these instances, the insured event is quite simple. Under life insurance, for example, the only question to be determined is whether the insured is dead.

As if all that were not bad enough, there is a second variable in any tort suit that makes it even more of a nightmare of complexity. The law starts from the premise that someone guilty of a tort—a tortfeasor (lawyers, too, have their impenetrable language)—is a wrongdoer, an evil person. That once was the case. Prior to the industrial age, most tortfeasors *were* evil people. Before the advent of machines, it was difficult to injure another without intending to. With machines, however, inadvertent injuries have become the norm. But because tort law started from the premise of a wrongdoer who had wronged an innocent party, the injured party was allowed to recover not only for medical expenses and wage loss but also for the monetary "value" of pain. It is difficult enough to ascertain exactly the wages a person has lost and will lose and what his medical expenses are and will be. What, however, is the monetary value of physical agony? What is an aching back worth? There is no rational answer to that—no "market" for aching backs. Nor can we turn to the financial pages and find a functioning market that tells us what a scar on the forehead is going for or what the loss of a leg is worth in indignity and denial of pleasure. So what does the law do? It delegates that question to juries, with the plaintiffs' lawyers using harps and violins and other "scientific" instruments to convey the value of the loss, with juries given almost unlicensed discretion to squander or stint through whim or bias. So females get more for pain and suffering than males for the same injury, and older persons get more than younger ones. There is no real reason behind it all; no evidence that females suffer more than males. Once again, trying to rationalize all this under economic principles is difficult, indeed.

Note that in paying for noneconomic loss, tort liability insurance once again is unlike any other form of insurance. When a person dies, a life insurance company does not pay for the surviving spouse's grief, although lawyers could have a field day litigating just how much the spouses loved—or hated—each other. No, the face amount of the policy is paid—no more, no less, regardless of love, hate, or indifference. Similarly, health insurance doesn't pay a mother for her pain in labor (though pain there surely is); rather only the reasonable obstetrical expenses are paid. And when a person's house burns down, fire insurance does not pay for the pain of losing a structure built by one's grandfather with his own hands two generations ago; no, only the face amount of the policy is payable.

Once one understands how wildly complex tort liability insurance is compared to every other form of insurance in having to determine who or what was at fault and the monetary value of nonmonetary loss, one can better understand why such insurance is such a mess and why it is so uniquely fraught with litigation, delay, and uncertainty. One can even appreciate that quite apart from whether tort liability insurance happens to be readily available at a reasonable price at any given time in the market, the system should be changed—although, obviously, high costs and unavailability highlight the need for change.

There is a third variable in tort law that also grew out of a view of the tortfeasor as an evil person, a wrongdoer. When Smith injures Jones and Jones is covered by health insurance (or disability insurance or life insurance) to a very substantial degree, Smith is not allowed (nor is the judge or jury) to take account of the fact that Jones has already been paid for a good deal of his economic loss. Smith must pay all over again. So either Jones is paid twice or his health insurer, which has already borne the loss, must pursue a complicated subrogation claim against Smith to recoup the amount already covered by insurance. As a result, the tort liability system is unleashed to bear the cost that society has already borne, either through private or social insurance, on the grounds that it would be unthinkable to allow the wrongdoer to benefit by insurance already covering the loss.

Once again, other forms of insurance for injury or property damage do not pay—or, actually, overpay—regardless of other forms of insurance that are payable. Health and disability and fire insurance policies, for example, are careful to provide for proration of payment among the applicable insurance policies, precisely to avoid any possibility of overpayment and resultant waste—and even chicanery (see chapter 6).

Finally, tort law decrees that any form of payment will be made in one lump sum, necessitating a hazardous prediction of the duration of further medical bills and wage loss indefinitely into the future—a guess doomed to be almost inevitably wrong when, as is often the case, medical prognosis is uncertain. Again, no other form of insurance for continuing losses—health or disability or workers' compensation insurance, for example—decrees such a rigid and unrealistic form of payment. Rather, other forms of insurance sensibly provide for periodic payment as loss accrues. (Granted that under so-called structured settlements, the parties to a tort suit can and often do agree to periodic payment, but either party can obstruct that sensible arrangement, as often happens.)

The result is a system that, as legal academics since the 1930s have pointed out, is a nightmare, despite its intuitive appeal. The result, as we have seen, is a system in which many deserving victims are not paid anything because they cannot prove that someone or something was at fault, even though in fact that may have been the case, and many others are paid a small fraction of their loss because they can't afford the years of delay until the matter is settled. These injured persons, with mounting medical expenses and wage losses, are often pressured into settling their cases with a tremendous discount against the delay that a jury trial would entail. The settlement process itself is so cumbersome that they usually are paid only years after the event. For example, the average delay in settling a product liability claim is about two years from the event—two years!—whereas it takes, on the average, one month to get a health insurance claim paid. Thus, for tort claims, seriously injured people wait in angst and uncertainty for years to find out if they will be paid, what they will be paid, and when they will be paid. And when paid, because of all the complexity involved—which calls for very skillful expertise on the part of counsel and others—the injured party will be forced to turn over a third or a half or even 60 percent of what he is awarded for litigation expenses and counsel fees.

Studies indicate that for medical malpractice claims, only twenty-eight cents of the medical malpractice insurance dollar actually go to the victims of malpractice. The rest go to insurance overhead and legal fees. For product liability the portion is about thirty-three cents. That is a huge transaction cost, to use the jargon of the economist.

The answer to all this for work-place accidents, as we saw earlier, is workers' compensation. It was instituted about 100 years ago by Bismarck, of all people—not exactly the most enlightened figure in the history of Western Civilization in the last hundred years. But the tort system was too much for even Bismarck to stomach. If only to defuse the progressive movement sweeping Germany, Bismarck instituted reforms of all kinds, including those mandating social insurance. The most significant was workers' compensation, covering the first great wave of accidents to engulf modern society. It turned out to be quite a simple solution to the industrial accidents raging in Germany, England, the United States and throughout the industrialized world. Workers' compensation—a form of no-fault insurance enacted in Germany in the 1880s then in Britain in the 1890s and in the United States roughly between 1910 and 1920—decrees that when an employee is injured in the course of employment, he needn't sue, alleging that his employer was at fault and that he himself was free from fault, with all the litigation that entails. Rather, the employee is paid automatically for his medical expenses and is compensated in part for his wage loss. But not all of his wage loss. Typically, the maximum benefit for wage loss today is in the vicinity of $200 or $300 a week—a social insurance level. But that much is assured to the victim, regardless of how the accident happened, regardless of whether he was or was not at fault, regardless of whether he had on safety goggles, regardless of whether he had used the guard on the machine properly, regardless of whether the employer had or had not maintained the machine properly. Because the accident occurred in the course of employment, the loss is payable as an actuarially predictable and inevitable result of the industrial activity. But nothing is paid for pain and suffering. With no litigation over fault or pain and suffering, at a stroke the two litigious issues that plague tort liability are eliminated—the result is a relatively healthy, functioning insurance mechanism.

Admittedly, there are problems with workers' compensation. It doesn't work as well as the reformers said it would. (Things often don't work as well as we reformers say they will. Keep that in mind always.) But it has worked magnificiently compared to the tort system. In the switch for work-place accidents from tort liability to workers' compensation, society switched from its worst form of insurance for injury to its best. Under no other form of insurance that is widely applicable across society are so many victims of misfortune assured of unlimited (in both duration and time) medical benefits, including rehabilitation, plus wage loss of unlimited duration. There is no pressure anywhere in the world to replace workers' compensation with the tort system it replaced.

The next great wave of modern accidents was from automobiles. And again, as we have seen (chapter 11), no-fault insurance is the obvious answer to tort liability for auto accidents.

And why not, for that matter, no fault-insurance for all kinds of accidents—those from medical treatment, from malfunctioning products, and from such governmental services as police, fire, and park departments? As indicated earlier, the malfunctionings of the insurance mechanism for non-auto accidents are even worse than for auto accidents, because the insured event is much more complicated. Jim Dooley, a wily old trial lawyer who was on the Illinois Supreme Court, used to say that he could take a reasonably articulate Irish bartender and teach him to try an intersection auto accident case in about a day and a half. But the brightest lawyer in the world can't be taught quickly to try a medical malpractice case. It is a long, bruising process—he would have to learn enough medicine to cross-examine a doctor and make him look wrong. (Actually, that is not as hard as it sounds, but it's hard.) Because learning to try such cases takes such an effort and skill, medical malpractice cases are extremely demanding to prepare—as are product liability cases. However, even though the need for no-fault insurance in such cases may be great, it's also much harder to apply.

If you go into an auto accident in reasonably good shape and come out with a terrible gash on your forehead or even a severed leg, it isn't very hard to determine that it was the automobile accident that caused the gash or the amputation. But if you go to a health care provider for treatment, the law cannot decree that the health care provider must automatically pay you for any adverse conditions that appear after the treatment. Some adverse conditions may be due not to the treatment but to your presenting complaint. It may be that no matter what the doctor did, you were going to get worse. After all, you were sick when you went to the doctor in the first place, weren't you? Thus, separating the adverse conditions due to the treatment from those due to your presenting complaint is a most vexing question, even on a no-fault basis. A provision that every health care provider will be liable for all the adverse results occurring from medical service would be an unmanageable no-fault criterion; it would force health care providers to face unknowable new claims and costs.

The same is true of product injuries. Can the law decree that anybody who produces or sells or even possesses a product will pay for any injuries to third persons resulting from that product? What if you go to your neighbor's house and you slip and fall and smash your head on his marble table? On a no-fault basis, who pays for your resulting brain damage or paralysis? Does your neighbor pay as a homeowner? Does the marble quarry pay for it? Does the person who designed the table pay for it? Does the retailer pay for it? And if so, in what proportions does each pay once the law has abandoned a fault criterion? As we have seen under present law, it is hard enough to single out the person who was at fault and make him pay. If the table was defectively designed, then under present law at least the person who designed it supposedly can be made to pay (admittedly only after cumbersome litigation). But it is impossible as a practical matter for the law to decree who is going to pay for such a product injury under no-fault insurance. Assume further you trip over a book and break your leg. Does the publisher pay you? He was involved, as a causal factor, wasn't he? Once fault is not a factor, why not? So the whole problem of moving away from the moorings of fault and then deciding who pays becomes very tangled indeed, threatening potential defendants with unmanageable new claims and costs.

On the other hand, that doesn't mean that society must be left with the tort system, either as it exists or as it would be reformed according to the urging of insurance companies and their institutional insureds. The key to workers' compensation and auto no-fault reforms, unlike those being proposed by corporate and professional interests, was a *balanced* approach. The injured party finds it easier to be paid but gets paid less. That makes for a fair trade for both sides. If we cannot today adopt a complete no-fault system for non–work-place and nonauto accidents—for all the reasons just discussed—we at least can achieve some of the same trade-offs.

We should start from the following criteria for insurance reform for such accidents: (1) *to make it easier, to the maximum extent feasible, for injured persons to be paid promptly for their economic loss without litigating their own or others' fault and without significantly increasing current liability costs;* and (2) *to hold the line on—and perhaps even lower—costs by paying for any increase in new claims by lower litigation expense and lower payments for noneconomic loss.*

Under these criteria, the proposals from the insurance industry—or, in early 1986, the Reagan administration—to simply limit the rights of injured people (by limits on pain and suffering, contingent fees, joint and several liability, and so on)—do not pass muster. They leave us in every case with the unmanageable bases for payment that make us want to change the system in the first place—namely, being required to determine fault and pay for pain and suffering (albeit with upper limits). They also do little or nothing about abuses in minor cases leading to padding of claims and ambulance chasing. At the same time, by lessening the exposure of the defendants to large verdicts, they give less incentives to defendants to offer as substantial settlements as are made today in serious cases. If a defendant thinks he may have to pay a verdict that includes $2 million in pain and suffering damages, he is much more likely to settle for a claimant's $1 million in medical expenses and wage loss than if he knows pain and suffering damages are limited to $250,000. Such reforms, then, make it no easier—and often would make it harder—for injured persons to be paid promptly for their losses. But at the other end of the spectrum, proposals to obligate defendants to pay any and all claims—or at last an indeterminate number of new ones—on a no-fault basis cannot be guaranteed to avoid significantly increasing liability costs. Can we really ask those doctors paying $100,000 a year or so in medical malpractice premiums to cough up a lot more under a new and untried no-fault insurance scheme?

With these constraints in mind, we propose a new law that tries to meet the foregoing criteria for reform and thereby avoid the problems plaguing other reforms—namely, (1) litigating fault; (2) litigating, and paying for, the value of pain and suffering; (3) paying for losses already covered by other insurance; (4) paying in a lump sum, as opposed to periodically; and (5) facing unknowable new costs from paying on a no-fault basis.

The bill, which might be termed "neo-no-fault," proposes the following: Any defendant of a personal injury claim is given the option of offering to a claimant within 180 days periodic payment of the claimant's net economic loss (relatively prompt payment compared to the tort system). That payment will cover any medical expenses, including rehabilitation, and wage loss, beyond any health or disability insurance already payable to the claimant. (Also payable is a reasonable hourly fee for the claimant's lawyer.) Note that such benefits are generous compared to most health insurance policies, since few health insurance policies cover rehabilitation and most have severe upper limits on coverage. If a defendant in a tort suit promptly offers to pay these amounts to the claimant, that will foreclose further pursuit of a tort claim. In other words, the claimant is forced to accept such an offer. Indeed one might term the proposal, "Offers That Can't Be Refused." (Offers could be refused, however, when the defendant had acted intentionally or when the victim's economic losses were minimal, as with the death of a nonearner.)

Note that under this proposal, no defendant is *forced* to offer such a settlement; this avoids imposing unmanageable new burdens on potential defendants. But why *force* claimants to accept such a settlement? After all, today either party can settle—or offer to settle—for economic loss, with no payment for pain and suffering, no duplication of other payable insurance, and no further argument over fault. If parties are already free to agree to such a settlement, why should the law *force* the plaintiff to accept such an offer from a defendant?

In answer to that, the best settlement of most personal injury claims would seem to be—as under workers' compensation or no-fault auto insurance—prompt, sure, periodic payment of the injured person's economic loss, as opposed to the tort system and its mere chance at a long-delayed lump sum that is likely to be either greater or less than the real loss. Yet such settlements do not often arise today. Defendants (or their insurers) rarely make early offers as generous as a commitment to cover all of an injury victim's economic loss, past and future. Defendants fear that making such an offer would only encourage claimants to believe that they can recover even more if they persevere through litigation. Thus, defendants often fail to offer prompt settlement for the claimant's net economic loss, even when, at first blush, it might be thought advantageous for them to do so.

And if defendants did make such a settlement offer, claimants or their lawyers frequently would reject it, because they would see it as a sign—as defendants rightly fear they would—that the case is worth much more. So the lottery aspect of the present system and the possibility of a very large recovery combine to spur on plaintiffs—and especially their attorneys. *Especially their attorneys*, because the role of the plaintiffs' attorneys cannot be underestimated. Constantly tempted by the "big hit," they have an incentive to take the case to trial, to risk the chance of recovering nothing for the opportunity to strike it rich. Plaintiffs' attorneys typically have a number of contingency-fee clients and thus are able to spread the risk of a poor or even no recovery over all of them. The plaintiff, on the other hand, does not have this "portfolio diversification," and his ability to recover is wrapped up in only one case—his own.

For these and other reasons, there is a reluctance both to initiate and to respond to offers of settlement for net economic loss. The plaintiff, also, fears sending a signal of weakness to the opposing party by such an offer of settlement.

How can we get around this mutual intransigence, that is encouraged by the vague and amorphous criteria of tort liability? We have seen that we cannot eliminate the intransigence on both sides by passing a no-fault statute that is applicable to all injuries and that requires both sides to accept disposal of the case by prompt payment of economic loss for fear of unknowable numbers of new claims. Nor can we define the insured event very well in advance for many medical or product injuries. On the other hand, we cannot force a defendant to pay any claim for economic loss made to him by a claimant, because any claimant could then make a claim against almost anyone and procure payment. For example, if Jones were to be victimized by a hit-and-run driver, he could just call up the registry of motor vehicles, get some license plate numbers, and make a claim against the owners of those vehicles—and they would be required to pay his economic loss! This is obviously an unworkable scheme. But it is *not* unworkable to provide that once a defendant has had time to examine a claim, he would be allowed to require the claimant to accept payment of net economic losses in total satisfaction of the claim.

When would a defendant be inclined to do so? If the defendant, after examining the claim, decides, for example, that the claimant never was in its hospital or never used its product, the defendant would not tender net economic loss—not only because defending and defeating the claim would be easy but also because it would be important for moral reasons to deny the claim. It's also important for the defendant to avoid getting a reputation as an easy target for spurious or marginal claims. On the other hand, consider a claim that the defendant thinks it might be able to defeat but that *is* a claim by its patient or by a user of its product for an adverse condition that clearly occurred as a result of a stay in the defendant's hospital or the use of the defendant's product. Although the defendant may not believe the accident was its fault, it would determine what it would cost to pay the claimant periodically for his medical expense and wage loss and, if that sum turns out to be less than what the defendant would have to pay on defense lawyers' fees plus tort damages, including payment for pain and suffering, the defendant would have found a good trade. Indeed, in many cases, what the defendant would spend solely in lawyers' fees might be more than the cost of paying the claimant's net economic loss. And in some cases, the defendant's wish to avoid all the bitterness of adversary litigation, both in courtroom battles and in the prolonged preparation therefore, may tip the scales in favor of such an offer to pay economic losses even if it might cost somewhat more.

What about the risk that such a law might give defendants an unfair advantage by allowing them to settle for claimants' economic losses in cases in which defendants would be obliged to pay much more in a tort suit while never forcing them to settle for more than they would pay in such a suit? Given the huge costs of defending tort cases and the gamble of large payment for noneconomic losses, defendants would be prompted to offer noneconomic losses not just in cases they are sure to lose but even in many—perhaps most—cases in which the issue of liability is in doubt. One leading defense lawyer hypothesizes that of the 250 cases his office then was defending, all in various stages of litigation, he would advise making an offer to pay claimants' net economic losses in 200 of them if the bill were to pass.

What about claimants? Would they be disadvantaged by this new law? The answer is that most claimants are already unhappy with the slugfest tort lawyers have created. Few persons who have been seriously injured have any taste for (1) a lottery to determine whether their medical expenses and wage loss will be paid and (2) a bitter fight that constantly reminds them of the accident—even to the point of being challenged by the other side's lawyer, often rather snidely, that a jury might consider them liars or cheats. Such battles may be acceptable to lawyers, who undertake them all the time, but the people they represent hate the process. Given the choice between a system that encourages prompt payment of real losses versus one that encourages a gamble for long-delayed, only possible payment of more, the certainty of prompt payment is the more attractive. The premise of the bill is that spending vast sums to guess at the responsibility for the accident and to pay some victims much more than their loss and many others much less is not nearly so wise as encouraging injured victims to be compensated promptly. Prompt payment to accident victims without litigation over who or what was at fault has the benign effect of lessening the psychic shock, strain, and subsequent traumatic neurosis often suffered by accident victims, as indicated in research conducted by Dr. Lester Keiser, chief of neuropsychiatry at Memorial Hospital, Hollywood, Florida. According to a report on Dr. Keiser's research:

> Under the old automobile insurance system with its frequent and lengthy lawsuits, the nervous strain experienced by an accident victim is often intensified in the ensuing wrangles with claim adjustors and lawyers.... [Some individuals

become] so absorbed in nursing their symptoms and pressing their claims that they completely alter their lives. Dr. Keiser notes that no-fault insurance [enacted in his home state of Florida] obviously does not eliminate the inevitable emotional stress that follows an accident. But what it does do, he says, is eliminate many of the conditions that make such a trauma worse.[1]

Returning to our criteria for reform, this proposed reform would make it easier, to the maximum extent feasible, for injured persons to be paid promptly for their economic losses without litigating their own or others' fault and without significantly increasing current liability costs (by not forcing defendants to pay an unknowable number of new claimants). It also would hold the line on—and perhaps even lower—costs by assuring that the costs of any increase in new claims would be offset by lower litigation expenses and lower payments for noneconomic loss.

Trial lawyers and others may criticize the proposal on the grounds that it removes the deterrent effect of findings of fault and payment of damages for pain and suffering. There are several answers to that. First, the tort system is often arbitrary and capricious in imposing losses in such a way as to discourage rational deterrent behavior by potential defendants. Witness the vaccine experience. Moreover, criminologists have preached for years that in order to be effective as a deterrent, punishment must be swift and certain. And swift and certain are two things that tort law surely is not. In addition, whatever punishment is imposed by tort law is heavily diluted, if not obliterated, by being borne not by the supposedly guilty defendant but by all those who pay for similar insurance coverage. Finally, under this proposal, a tort claim is foreclosed only by offering to pay an injury victim's economic losses in perpetuity—a not insufficient commitment in itself. Defendants are by no means escaping scot-free under this plan. Under this neo-no-fault proposal, we do not abandon tort liability completely. Rather, in a sort of jujitsu maneuver, we use tort law's bulk and weight as leverage to spin it around to protect ourselves, thereby avoiding its crushing effects.

As for deterrence, we can gain a fascinating insight into how well tort law is supposed to deter substandard conduct by examining how judges view the impact of possible liability on themselves. Consider the case of *Stump v. Sparkman*, in which the U.S. Supreme Court ruled that an injured party had no redress against a judge who approved the sterilization of a 15-year-old girl at her mother's request, without letting the girl know or appointing anyone to represent her interests. Said the Court: "A judge will not be deprived of immunity [from suit] because the action he took was in error, was done maliciously, or was in excess of his authority." Even "grave procedural errors" give rise to no liability, despite "unfairness to litigants that sometimes result." The rationale is that there would be danger to "the judicial process" if judges (as well as prosecutors) have to worry about being sued. These are the same judges who increasingly order liability to be imposed on others, not only for malicious acts but for simply careless ones and even where there is no fault at all. Included in the ever-widening gambit of liability are manufacturers, doctors, government officials, and even police officers who make erroneous arrests and searches ordered by the immune judges! (Supposedly, all that liability is imposed on others to encourage them to act appropriately. Apparently, the contrast in their treatment of themselves and others is what judges mean by equal protection of the law.)

A version of the neo-no-fault proposal, applicable to medical malpractice, is before the U.S. Congress, introduced by Representatives Richard Gephardt (D.-Mo.) and Henson Moore (R.-La.) Another version, applicable only to surgery, was introduced before the Massachusetts legislature by Governor Michael Dukakis, an early supporter of no-fault auto insurance. Attempts to apply the idea to product liability are being pursued in federal legislation introduced by Senator John Danforth (R.-Mo).

One further variation of the proposal should be mentioned. The bill could provide that a claimant would have a choice in whether or not to accept the defendant's offer. But if the claimant refuses the offer of settlement and resorts to litigation, any amount that he or she might win in that litigation would be subject to a cap of, for example, $250,000 for pain and suffering. Thus, a cap would be imposed only when the plaintiff had been *offered* prompt compensation and the chance to avoid litigation. Thus, defendants would still have an incentive to make such offers of settlement—to trigger the cap mechanism if the victim rejected the settlement. Victims, in turn, would have an incentive to accept any offer that is made—to receive prompt payment—and this would be buttressed by the knowledge that if he or she resorted to litigation, any recovery would be subject to the cap. In this way, the chances of reaching a settlement—providing for fair compensation quickly and without litigation—would be increased. Unlike the usual proposals for caps, limitations on attorney's fees, and so forth, this idea would not impose restrictions across the board; it would not affect accident victims to whom an offer of settlement has not been made and who therefore must resort to litigation. Restrictions would only apply when victims have had an opportunity to avoid litigation through what society deems a fair settlement and have rejected it.

What are the prospects for such bills? As we have noted, trial lawyers, who will oppose them, are very powerful lobbyists. The personal injury bar is probably the most lucrative segment of the bar in the United States. There are lawyers in cities and towns all over this country who are making a million dollars a year and more from personal injury litigation. And they are practicing not only in major metropolises but also in places like Midland, Texas, or Fort Wayne, Indiana. Unlike most lawyers—who are admittedly well paid—personal injury lawyers are not tied to their time sheets. There is only so much you can charge anybody per hour—even IBM. But if a lawyer gets a third of a $3 million claim, along with the contingency fees in many other substantial personal injury cases in his pipeline, he has "a piece of the action" in a way that no other lawyer has. That explains why personal injury lawyers are so wealthy, why they have so much invested in the present system, and why they fight so ferociously to keep it. And that, in turn, is why it is so difficult to pass statutes that would change that system. Furthermore, the argument lawyers make in defense of the present system is not, on its face, pure nonsense. The way the tort system works may be nonsense—but not its underlying theory. Lawyers argue that it is immoral to treat the drunk and the sober, the careful and the careless equally. The fact that all payments are made out of large and impersonal pools of insurance dollars, and that other forms of insurance—life, health, accident, and fire insurance—*do* treat the drunk, the sober, the careful, and the careless in the same way would seem to undercut that argument. But lawyers' political power and the complexity of the arguments for reform—coupled with the difficulty of getting *any* statute passed in this country, especially a controversial one—make legislative reform uncertain at best.

Another factor is that there are numerous good causes to which concerned legislators can devote time and energy—child abuse, the impoverished state of the arts, and so on. In Pat Moynihan's words, "This is a world of competing sorrows." Even if one can get the attention of such legislators, one cannot be at all sure that what the legislature eventually enacts will make any sense. The resulting legislation, after all the pulling and pushing of various interests, may look like the proverbial camel designed by a committee—with humps and dips one never predicted. If you want to suffer, go watch a bill you are interested in being debated in a legislature, and watch the horse-trading that goes on. A clause that is absolutely essential to the bill may go out, and the bill may then go sailing through in a form that is inimical to your purpose in trying to get it passed in the first place. And once a bill has been passed, getting it repealed is that much harder. You've had your turn; now the legislature must turn to someone else's "sorrow." Our experience with no-fault auto insurance has taught us this lesson with a vengeance.

What about alternatives to legislation, then? Not that legislation should not be pursued—but one should have alternatives.

In this connection, Doug McBroom's $6.3 million jury award for Chris Thompson against the Seattle School District (see chapter 1) sent shock waves through school systems across the nation. Convinced for all the reasons just mentioned that legislative reform was not readily available, the National Federation of High School Athletic Associations, through its insurance broker, Doug Ruedlinger of Topeka, Kansas, approached the senior author of this book to try to find a nonlegislative solution to the schools' miseries. As a result, a contract was drafted that closely resembles the aforementioned bill but with a crucial difference: under the contract, an insurer guarantees to a school district at the start of the school year that when an athlete is catastrophically injured (defined as injury leading to more than $25,000 of loss), the insurer will offer, within ninety days, to pay for all of the student's net economic loss, medical expenses, and rehabilitation, and $300 a week for wage loss—periodically as loss accrues—without regard to any tort liability on the part of the school for causing the accident. As under the proposed statutes, nothing is payable for pain and suffering, nor does payment duplicate amounts already paid to the student from another source, such as health insurance. The student and his family are then given a further ninety days to accept these benefits and waive their right to sue on the basis of tort—or to sue. As a result, the student has the alternative of prompt payment of real losses, rather than years of uncertainty.

Because this program is instituted by contract, however, not by statute, the student's tort rights can be surrendered only by his agreement, not by legislative command. This created a problem for insurers. When they first looked at the plan, they were worried that athletes with good claims would proceed with their tort claims and those with bad tort claims would accept the no-fault benefits, with the result that costs would skyrocket. But the premise of the contract was that seriously injured people are averse to the risks of litigation, so if an insurer came to such a victim promptly after the accident and made such a tender—so long as the offer was not a signal of a weak case—the tenders would be accepted. This is a very important point. Note that under this contract, plaintiffs and their lawyers cannot perceive the offer to pay net economic loss as a signal of weakness. The insurer makes the offer not because it fears liability but because it bound itself to make that offer at the start of the school year, before it could know anything about the accident. Thus, the threat to take the offer off the table in ninety days is a very real one. Indeed, a lawyer who advises rejecting the offer may be looking at a malpractice case against himself.

The plan is in effect in forty-eight states, covering more than 60 percent of all high schools, at a cost of $1.25 per student-athlete. In the twenty-six cases of serious injury in which the program has been applied so far, every accident victim but one has agreed to accept the tender of benefits and to waive any right to sue on the basis of tort. Thus, whereas Chris Thompson, the 15-year-old Seattle student, waited years to settle his paralysis claim (chapter 1), when Marty Wittman, a 16-year-old Seattle athlete, later suffered a similar accident, he had a very different experience. Wittman was left paralyzed from an interscholastic wrestling match. Whereas Thompson waited and waited for payment, Wittman and his family benefited shortly after his accident from the aforementioned insurance policy (created, ironically, because of the lawsuit Thompson had filed and won). Wittman, who was hospitalized for six months following the injury and then underwent rehabilitation for two days a week on an outpatient basis, was the first beneficiary of the new insurance policy. In addition to prompt payment of all related medical expenses, Marty Wittman received a new van, modified to include hand controls and a wheelchair lift. The Wittman home was also remodeled to accommodate his condition. Unlike Thompson, Wittman did not have to "roll the dice in the courtroom," to use Doug McBroom's description of Chris Thompson's experience.

In a similar case, on the opening kickoff of the Nebraska High School football championships in November 1983, Jerry Ediger tackled the ball carrier and dislocated two vertebrae, becoming a quadriplegic as a result. Rather than waiting in uncertainty, the Ediger family's soaring medical bills for months of hospital care and physical therapy, as well as the costs of installing wheelchair ramps and a hospital bathtub in the family's Henderson, Nebraska, farmhouse, were covered by the new contract. According to John Ediger, Jerry's father, "We'd have managed, but I don't know how. We'd have had to borrow a lot of money without [the plan]."[2]

Could such a plan be adapted to medical malpractice, product liability, and other forms of insurance? It would be more difficult than it was for athletic injuries. The contract, unlike a statute, requires that the insured event be defined in advance, which is impossible in many cases of medical and product injuries. But there are many injuries from health care and malfunctioning products that *could* be identified in advance and incorporated into a similar contract. Admittedly, the difficulties of having defendants oblige themselves in advance to pay for accidents on a no-fault basis will mean that the contractual device will not be applied as sweepingly as would a similar plan instituted by legislation. (For a comparison of the legislative and contractual "neo-no-fault" plans, see the appendix to this book.)

Professor Patrick Atiyah of Oxford University has summed up the case for the types of reforms urged here:

> Given the huge administrative costs of the tort system, and the extraordinary generosity of pain and suffering awards, it must be recognized that every expansion of tort law uses resources totally out of proportion to the numbers assisted by that expansion. If we could find a compensation system with [a low] . . . administrative cost—by no means an unreasonable ambition—and if we were willing to contemplate the elimination of compensation for pain and suffering, we could thus probably compensate, without additional costs, *four* accident victims for every *one* compensated today. . . . If we were willing to include ceilings and thresholds [on payment] as well, there is no doubt that we could quite easily afford to compensate a significant proportion of the pecuniary losses suffered by perhaps six, seven, or eight accident victims for every one protected by the tort system. . . . I will venture the prophecy that in fifty years time people will look back with some horror on tort law as a means of compensation that [thrived] . . . too long.[3]

In short, society ought to avoid, wherever feasible, "shin-kicking" litigation as a means of deciding whether injured people get paid by insurance. After all, it was shortly after the last turn of the century that our grandparents—with comparatively little information, actuarial or otherwise, to go on—abandoned tort liability as a means of paying injured employees. As to other types of injury, as we approach the next turn of the century surely we can follow (and thereby avoid) suit.[4]

Appendix: Neo-No-Fault Legislation and Contracts Compared and Combined

WHAT are the similarities and differences associated with the legislative and contractual "neo-no-fault" proposals proposed here? Under either umbrella, defendants offer to pay injured parties' net economic losses promptly as they accrue. But what are the comparable advantages and disadvantages of each approach? Are they mutually exclusive—or can they be coordinated?

If guaranteeing benefits for victims of medical and product injuries under a complete no-fault scheme is an idea seemingly posing insurmountable problems, that doesn't mean we cannot provide *many* such victims with such benefits, either by legislation or contract, or both.

In the case of the contractual neo-no-fault plan, the *injurer* is under a contractually self-imposed obligation to offer no-fault-like benefits, with the *injured* party having an option to accept the offer or not. In the case of the statutory plan, the *injured* party is under a legislatively imposed obligation to accept the offer of no-fault-like benefits, with the *injurer* having the option to offer the benefits or not.

Recall that a complete no-fault system for all victims, as under legislatively imposed workers' compensation, operates by giving neither side an option: the injurer must offer to pay the injured party's economic loss and the injured party must accept the offer. But, as pointed out, such an across-the-board no-fault approach is not feasible for many kinds of injuries from products and medical services. Under the common law, on the other hand, the injurer has the option of making or eschewing a post-accident offer to pay the injured party's economic loss (or any other amount), and the injured party has an option of accepting any offer or not. That system is not working.

So, if for some injuries we are not able to impose on both parties the no-fault alternative to common law claims of payment of certain but lesser benefits, but still want to change the common law system for such injuries, we revert to the two different approaches of (1) having the *injurer* under a contractual obligation make an offer of no-fault-like benefits, with the *injured* party having an option to refuse it, or (2) having the *injured* party under a statutory obligation accept the offer of no-fault-like benefits, with the *injurer* having an option to offer it.

Why the difference in who gets the option and what are the implications therefrom? Lacking a statute, there is no way that the injured party can be denied his right to refuse an offer of settlement. This explains the injured party's option under the contractual plan. But even by statute there is no workable way a defendant can be obligated to accept an offer of settlement by any claimant. Such a scheme would allow a claimant to make almost random claims and extract payments for such. This explains the injurer's option under the statutory plan.

Keep in mind the crucial factor: under both the legislative and contractual proposals, the offer to pay net economic loss is *not* a signal of weakness in the defendant's case prompting the plaintiff to ask for more than net economic loss. Under the statutory plan, the plaintiff cannot turn down the offer; under the contractual plan, because the offer is made pursuant to a pre-accident commitment (before the circumstances of the accident could have been known), plaintiffs cannot assume the offer is a floor from which higher offers will later spring.

What are the advantages and disadvantages of the contractual versus the legislative approach when it comes to offering to pay claimants' net economic losses? The contractual approach avoids the pitfalls and frustration of passing legislation. It also assures that, once the potential injurer has made a precise commitment to offer to pay net economic loss for given injuries, the commitment will be met in any case covered by the pre-accident agreement. But because the commitment is made on a pre-accident basis (along with the claimant having a post-accident option to turn it down), there are formidable problems of comprehensively defining when no-fault benefits will be due. As a result, in many instances—especially for health care services—the occasions for prompt payment of economic loss may be relatively limited.

Also, the contractual plan appears unfeasible for any but serious injuries, thus leaving in place smaller, nuisance tort claims, with all the concomitant costs of such claims to society. Why? Because a claimant with relatively small economic loss is not under financial pressure to accept settlement for his net economic loss. It is not usually to his advantage to forego his right to claim in tort for relatively large amounts for pain and suffering, in return for the relatively small returns from prompt payment for economic loss which he can easily absorb anyway. Thus, the dollars currently being misspent on smaller, nuisance claims cannot be eliminated by the contractual device. This also means that a potential defendant cannot foreclose even serious tort claims of any type when the claimants' losses have already been largely met by collateral sources such as workers' compensation, accident and health insurance, or disability insurance. Here, too, as with the nuisance claim, payment of only net economic loss is not sufficiently attractive to induce the seriously injured (but collaterally covered) victim to forego his tort claim. But here, as with smaller nuisance claims, society nonetheless would arguably be well served by foreclosing expensive and cumbersome tort litigation when little economic loss has been suffered.

Conversely, this is precisely one of the things the statutory plan accomplishes—namely, the elimination of tort claims when relatively little economic loss has been suffered by a claimant. But a difficulty with the statutory plan, as previously suggested, is that the injurer may be wary of offering to pay net economic loss in cases where its tort defense looks feasible, thus leaving too much injury compensation to the vagaries of tort litigation.

Under which device will there be more tort claims—the contractual or the legislative plan? Hard to say. When the *injurer* has the option, nuisance claims will be foreclosed, as will claims in which legal fees and possible noneconomic damages and duplication of payments already made by Blue Cross or other insurers loom comparatively large. But injurers may not exercise their option as widely as one might hope. In other words, an injurer may be tempted to settle for the injured's net economic loss only in cases in which it would be obligated to pay much more at common law, while rarely if ever settling in other cases. On the other hand, when the *injured* have the option, all claims which the injurer has included in his election will be potentially covered. But because many injured parties may not exercise their option to accept the offer, the injurer may be tempted to exclude many claims from the definition of coverage. The important point, though, is that both plans offer incentives to use dollars to pay for net economic loss that were formerly misspent on many tort claims. So both approaches should be simultaneously pursued: contracts should be implemented and legislation lobbied for.

But won't passage of a well-drafted statute remove many incentives for potential defendants to contractually adopt pre-accident commitments to make post-accident offers? Why make such a pre-accident commitment (when by definition one is thereby flying somewhat blind) to make an offer that a claimant can turn down, when a statute allows one to make a post-accident offer (after all the circumstances of the accident are known) that a claimant *cannot* turn down?

The fact is a statutory scheme need not necessarily deter implementation of a contractual one. Consider that (1) a statutory scheme fails to compensate many by failing to provide a pre-accident guarantee, and (2) a contractual scheme fails to compensate many by requiring a pre-accident definition of compensable events. Thus, there is a need to marry the two schemes to supplement each other. How? The statute could provide that any party who offers to pay net economic loss pursuant to a pre-accident contractual commitment is entitled to be reimbursed from anyone also liable for the injury who offers to pay pursuant to a statute. Thus, if both a surgeon and an anesthesiologist were responsible for an injury to a patient, a surgeon paying for the patient's net economic loss pursuant to a contract would be entitled to shift the cost of paying for the net economic loss to the anesthesiologist, who in order to avoid liability for common law damages, including pain and suffering, offered to pay net economic loss pursuant to the statute. In this way there will still be a strong incentive to institute a pre-accident contractual guarantee to pay no-fault benefits, despite the existence of a statutory device merely permitting post-accident commitments to pay the same.[1]

Notes

SINCE this book is aimed at the general reader, the authors have generally limited footnotes to sources quoted at sufficient length to call for permission from the copyright holder thereof.

INTRODUCTION

1. "War Aftermath: $13.5 Million Award," *The New York Times*, August 31, 1982. Copyright © 1982 by The New York Times Company. Reprinted by permission.

1. RISKY GAMES—BEFORE AND AFTER INJURY

1. Larry Brown, "Mother of Quadriplegic Man Is Dying, Jurors Told," *The Seattle Times*, February 10, 1982, pp. A1, A21. Copyright © 1982 Seattle Times Co. Reprinted with permission.
2. Don Fair, "Second Tragedy in Football-Injury Suit," *Seattle Post Intelligencer*, February 11, 1982. Copyright © 1982 The Hearst Corporation. Reprinted with permission.
3. Ibid.
4. Larry Brown and Charles E. Brown, "Quadriplegic Gets $6.4 Million," *The Seattle Times*, February 12, 1982, p. A1.
5. Harry Brooks, "Thompson Will Strive for a Bright Future," *West Seattle Herald*, 1982. Copyright © 1982 West Seattle Herald. Reprinted with permission.
6. Dick Rockne, "Injured Gridder Still Waiting to Collect," *The Seattle Times*, July 22, 1983, pp. D1, D6. Copyright © Seattle Times Co. Reprinted with permission.

2. UNSETTLING SETTLEMENTS

1. Lawrence Van Gelder, "Nearly Blind Student Accepts $165,000, Forfeiting $900,000 Award From Jury," *The New York Times*, March 27, 1975, p. 1. Copyright © 1975 by The New York Times Company. Reprinted by permission.
2. Ibid., p. 20.
3. *The New York Times*, May 7, 1984, pp. A1, A15.
4. Francis J. Flaherty and David Lauter, "Inside Agent Orange: The 11th-Hour Talks That Almost Failed," and "Judge's Novel Rulings Spurred Settlement," *The National Law Journal*, May 21, 1984, pp. 1, 39–41. Copyright © 1984 New York Law Publishing Co. Reprinted with permission.

5. Ibid., p. 39.
6. Ibid.
7. Ibid.
8. Ibid., pp. 39–40.
9. Ibid., p. 40.
10. Ibid.
11. Ibid.
12. Ibid.
13. Ibid., p. 41.
14. *The New York Times*, May 7, 1984, p. A15.
15. Flaherty and Lauter, *supra* note 4, at 41. Still to come were some appeals by those not party to the settlement.

3. (MIS)TRIAL BY JURY

1. Elliot Cahn, "Winning Big Cases with Trial Simulations," *American Bar Association Journal*, Vol. 69, August 1983, p. 1073. Copyright © 1983 American Bar Association. Reprinted with permission from the *ABA Journal*, the Magazine of the Legal Profession.
2. Ibid., p. 1074.
3. Ibid., p. 1074.
4. Jeffrey O'Connell and Keith Carpenter, "Psychology and Trials: Some Disturbing Insights," *Missouri Law Review* 48 (Winter 1983): 300, copyright © 1983 The Curators of the University of Missouri, reprinted with permission; reviewing Norbert L. Kerr and Robert M. Bray, eds., *The Psychology of the Courtroom* (New York: Academic Press, 1982).
5. Earl C. Gottschalk, Jr., "While More Firms Try Jury Consultants, Debate Grows Over How Much They Help," *The Wall Street Journal*, April 3, 1981, p. 23. Reprinted by permission of *The Wall Street Journal*. © Dow Jones & Company, Inc., 1981. All Rights Reserved.
6. Ibid.
7. Ibid.
8. Ibid.
9. Ibid.
10. Judith Gonda, "How Insurers Can Use Litigation Psychology," *National Underwriter, Property & Casualty Edition*, March 4, 1983, p. 10. Reprinted with permission.
11. Ibid.
12. Ibid., p. 52.
13. Ibid.
14. Ibid.
15. Ibid.
16. Ibid.
17. Gottschalk, *supra* note 5.
18. Ibid.
19. Jonathan R. Laing, "For the Plaintiff: Lawyers Specializing in Personal-Injury Suits Find Business Is Good," *The Wall Street Journal*, August 2, 1972, p. 13. Reprinted by permission of *The Wall Street Journal*, © Dow Jones & Company, Inc., 1972. All Rights Reserved.

20. Jonathan R. Laing, "For the Defense: Keeping Verdicts Low in Personal-Injury Suits Takes Specialized Skills," *The Wall Street Journal*, July 5, 1973, p. 17. Reprinted by permission of *The Wall Street Journal*, © Dow Jones & Company, Inc., 1973. All Rights Reserved.
21. O'Connell and Carpenter, *supra* note 4, p. 311.

4. EXPERT CONFUSION

1. Tom Vesey, "More Experts Hiring Out As Witnesses," and related articles, *The Washington Post*, December 19, 1983, p. A14. Copyright © 1983 The Washington Post Company. Reprinted with permission.
2. Ibid.
3. Ibid.
4. Tamar Lewin, "Psychology and Law: An Experimental Marriage," *The New York Times*, May 16, 1982, p. E9. Copyright © 1982 by The New York Times Company. Reprinted by permission.
5. Ibid.
6. Ibid.
7. *New York Times*, July 28, 1981, p. B20.
8. Lewin, *supra* note 4.
9. John A. Jenkins, "Experts' Day in Court," *The New York Times Magazine*, December 11, 1983, p. 100. Copyright © 1983 by The New York Times Company. Reprinted by permission.
10. Ibid., p. 104.
11. Ibid., p. 98.
12. Ibid.
13. Ibid., p. 106.
14. Ibid.
15. Ibid.
16. Ibid., p. 102.
17. Ibid.
18. Quoted in Jenkins, *supra* note 9, at 100.
19. Ibid.
20. Ibid., p. 103.
21. Ibid., p. 98.
22. Vesey, *supra* note 1, p. A14.
23. Ibid.
24. Ibid.
25. Jenkins, *supra* note 9, at 102.
26. Vesey, *supra* note 1, at A14.
27. Jonathan R. Laing, "For the Plaintiff: Lawyers Specializing in Personal-Injury Suits Find Business Is Good," *The Wall Street Journal*, August 2, 1972, p. 13. Reprinted by permission of *The Wall Street Journal*. © Dow Jones & Company, Inc., 1972. All Rights Reserved.
28. Vesey, *supra* note 1, at A1.
29. Ibid.

30. Thomas E. Silfen, "When a Trial Lawyer Is on a Jury," *The Washington Post*, August 26, 1983, p. A17. Copyright © 1983 The Washington Post. Reprinted with permission.
31. Ibid.
32. Ibid.
33. Ibid.
34. Ibid.

5. THE LITIGATION LOTTERY

1. William Raspberry, "Taking an Edge," *The Washington Post*, November 12, 1984, p. A19. Copyright © 1984 The Washington Post Company. Reprinted with permission.
2. Michael Specter, "Watts Tragedy: An End to Mother's Inner Strength," *The Washington Post*, July 12, 1985, p. C1. Copyright © 1985 The Washington Post Company. Reprinted with permission.
3. Ibid.
4. Ibid.
5. Michael Specter, "Woman Slays Crippled Son and Then Self," *The Washington Post*, July 11, 1985, p. C2. Copyright © The Washington Post Company. Reprinted with permission.
6. Specter, *supra* note 2, at C6.
7. Ibid.
8. Ibid.
9. Dena Kleinman, "Malpractice Suit Gives Millions But Not Hope," *The New York Times*, March 11, 1985, p. B5. Copyright © 1985 The New York Times Company. Reprinted by permission.
10. Ibid.
11. Ibid.
12. Ibid.
13. Ibid.
14. Ibid.
15. Ibid.
16. Ibid.
17. Ibid., p. B1.
18. Ibid.
19. Ibid., p. B5.
20. Ibid., p. B1.
21. Ibid., p. B5.
22. Ibid.
23. Ibid., p. B1.
24. Ibid.
25. Editorial, "Taking the Law for a Subway Ride," *The New York Times*, December 27, 1983, p. A22. Copyright © 1983 by The New York Times Company. Reprinted by permission.
26. Ibid.
27. Richard Godosky, "When It Pays for the T.A. to Settle a Suit," *The New York Times* (letter to the editor), January 21, 1984, p. 20. Copyright © 1984 by The New York Times Company. Reprinted by permission.

28. Laura A. Kiernan, "Quadriplegic Battles for Help in Paying Accident Cost," *The Washington Post*, January 2, 1983, p. C1. Copyright © 1983 by The Washington Post Company. Reprinted with permission.
29. Ibid., p. C15.
30. Ibid.
31. Ibid.
32. Ibid.
33. Ibid.
34. Ibid.
35. Ed Bruske, "Starting Over," *The Washington Post*, January 31, 1983, p. B7. Copyright © 1983 by The Washington Post Company. Reprinted with permission.
36. Ibid.
37. Ibid.
38. Ibid.
39. Ibid., p. B1.

6. FROM WRECKS TO RICHES

1. Information on Chicago auto cases from "The Accident Swindlers," a series in *Chicago Sun-Times*, February 10–24, 1980 ©. Reprinted with permission of Chicago Sun-Times.
2. Ibid., February 15, 1980.
3. Ibid.
4. Ibid.
5. Ibid., February 10, 1980.
6. Ibid.
7. Ibid.
8. Ibid.
9. Ibid.
10. Alfred G. Haggerty, "Insurer Gears Up to Brake Phony Auto Accident Scams," *National Underwriter, Property & Casualty Edition*, July 27, 1984, p. 3. Reprinted with permission.
11. Ibid., p. 2.
12. Ibid.
13. Ibid.
14. Jane Berentson, "Integrity Test: Five of Thirteen Lawyers Fail," *American Lawyer*, May 1980, p. 15. Copyright © 1980 AM-LAW Publishing Corp. Reprinted with permission.
15. Ibid.
16. Ibid.
17. Ibid.
18. Ibid.
19. Ibid., p. 16.
20. Ibid.
21. Ibid.
22. Ibid., p. 17.
23. Ibid., p. 18.
24. Ibid., p. 16.
25. Ibid., pp. 16–17.

26. "The Accident Swindlers," *supra* note 1, February 11, 1980.
27. Ibid.
28. Ibid.
29. Ibid.
30. Ibid.
31. Ibid.
32. Ibid., February 20, 1980.
33. Ibid., February 17, 1980.
34. Ibid.
35. Ibid.
36. Ibid.
37. Ibid.
38. Ibid.
39. Ibid., February 24, 1980.
40. Ibid.
41. Ibid., February 12, 1980.
42. Ibid., February 14, 1980.
43. Ibid., February 15, 1980.
44. Ibid.
45. Ibid.
46. Selwyn Raab, "Former Lawyer Says He Paid Off Judges In Medical Lawsuits," *The New York Times*, March 7, 1985, p. B7. Copyright © 1985, by The New York Times Company. Reprinted by permission.
47. Ibid.
48. Ibid.

7. THE INJURED CITIZENRY

1. Robert Lindsey, "Businesses Change Ways in Fear of Lawsuits," *The New York Times*, November 18, 1985, p. B7. Copyright © 1985 by The New York Times Company. Reprinted by permission.
2. Eric Pianin, "Funds Sought to Cover Lawsuits Against District," *The Washington Post*, May 6, 1985, p. C1. Copyright © The Washington Post Company. Reprinted with permission.
3. Ibid., p. C7.
4. Robert Lindsey, "Lawsuits' Surge Strains Budgets of Many Cities," *The New York Times*, May 12, 1985, p. 28. Copyright © 1985 by The New York Times Company. Reprinted by permission.
5. Ibid.
6. Ibid.
7. Ibid.
8. Ibid.
9. Ibid.
10. Ibid.
11. Ibid.
12. Ibid.
13. Laurie McGinley, "Explosive Growth of Lawsuits Against the U.S. Creates Concern

Over Potential Budget Impact," *The Wall Street Journal*, January 14, 1985, p. 38. Reprinted by permission of The Wall Street Journal, © Dow Jones & Company, Inc., 1985. All Rights Reserved.
14. Ibid.
15. Ibid.
16. Ibid.
17. Ibid.
18. Ibid.
19. Ted Gest and Ronald Taylor with Mary Galligan and Ron Scherer, "Product-Liability Suits: Why Nobody Is Satisfied," *U.S. News & World Report*, August 19, 1985, p. 49. Copyright © 1985 U.S. News & World Report. Reprinted with permission.
20. McGinley, *supra* note 13, at 38.
21. "Colleges Facing Insurance Crisis," UPI wire report in *The Washington Post*, September 30, 1985, p. D4. Copyright © 1985 The Washington Post Company. Reprinted with permission.
22. Sandra Sugawara, "Day Care Insurance Imperiled," *The Washington Post*, July 19, 1985, p. C7. Copyright © 1985 The Washington Post Company. Reprinted with permission. See also *The New York Times*, July 19, 1985, p. A15.
23. Jay Mathews, "Day Care Centers Find Insurance Unavailable." *The Washington Post*. May 12, 1985, p. A4. Copyright © 1985 The Washington Post Company. Reprinted with permission.
24. Ibid.
25. Joe Taylor, "Schools, Governments See Huge Insurance Rate Increases," *The Daily Progress* (Charlottesville, Va.), November 21, 1985, p. B3. Used by permission of the Associated Press.
26. Ibid.
27. Ibid.
28. Ibid.
29. Gest and Taylor, *supra* note 19, at 50.
30. Stuart Taylor, Jr., "Product Liability: The New Morass," *The New York Times*, March 10, 1985, sec. 3, p. 9. Copyright © 1985 by The New York Times Company. Reprinted by permission.
31. Ibid., p. 8.
32. Ibid.

8. MEDICAL MALPRACTICE'S MALPRACTICE

1. Carol Lawson, "Midwives Facing Loss of Insurance," *The New York Times*, June 13, 1985, p. C3. Copyright © 1985 by The New York Times Company. Reprinted by permission.
2. Ibid.
3. Sharon Johnson, "Malpractice Costs vs. Health Care for Women," *The New York Times*, July 19, 1985, p. A14. Copyright © 1985 by The New York Times Company. Reprinted by permission.
4. Andrew H. Malcolm, "Fear of Malpractice Suits Leading Some Doctors to Quit Obstetrics," *The New York Times*, February 12, 1985, p. D23. Copyright © 1985 by The New York Times Company. Reprinted by permission.

5. Ibid.
6. Ibid.
7. Ibid.
8. Ivan K. Strausz, "How to Drive Doctors Out," *The New York Times*, April 8, 1985, p. A17. Copyright © 1985 by The New York Times Company. Reprinted by permission.
9. Ibid.
10. Johnson, *supra* note 3, at A14.
11. Ibid.
12. Ibid.
13. Ibid.
14. Ibid.
15. Ibid.
16. Strausz, *supra* note 8, at A17.
17. *Newsweek*, April 29, 1985, p. 58.
18. N.R. Kleinfield, "The Malpractice Crunch at St. Paul," *The New York Times*, February 24, 1985, p. F4. Copyright © 1985 by The New York Times Company. Reprinted by permission.
19. Ibid.
20. Ibid.
21. Ibid.
22. Ibid.
23. Ibid.
24. Ibid.
25. Tamar Lewin, "Pharmaceutical Companies Are the Hardest Hit," *The New York Times*, March 10, 1985, sec. 3, p. 9. Copyright © 1985 by The New York Times Company. Reprinted by permission.
26. Ibid., p. 1.
27. Ibid.
28. Ibid., p. 9.
29. Ibid.
30. Ibid.
31. Ibid.
32. Ibid.
33. Strausz, *supra* note 8, at A17.

9. WHEN GOODS GO BAD

1. Andrew Hacker, "The Asbestos Nightmare," *Fortune*, January 20, 1986, p. 121, copyright © 1986 Time, Inc., reprinted with permission; reviewing Brodeur, *Outrageous Misconduct: The Asbestos Industry on Trial* (New York, Pantheon, 1985).
2. Ibid., p. 125.
3. Ibid.
4. Ibid., p. 127.
5. Edmund W. Kitch, "Vaccines and Product Liability: A Case of Contagious Litigation," *Regulation*, May/June 1985, p. 14. Copyright © 1985 American Enterprise Institute. Reprinted by permission of *Regulation* magazine.

6. Ibid., p. 15.
7. Ibid.
8. Ibid.
9. Ibid., pp. 16–17.
10. Ibid., p. 17. Information on recent increase in price of DPT vaccine from *The Washington Post,* May 23, 1986, p. A14.
11. Kitch, *supra* note 5.
12. Ibid., p. 18.

10. REFORMING REFORMS

1. See *Report of the Tort Policy Working Group on the Cause, Extent and Policy Implications of the Current Crisis in Insurance Availability and Affordability* (Washington, D.C., February 1986).
2. "Sorry, Your Policy Is Cancelled," *Time,* March 24, 1986, p. 26. Copyright © 1986 Time, Inc. Reprinted with permission.
3. Ibid.
4. Steven Brostoff, "New Consumer Group Against Tort Reforms," *National Underwriter, Property & Casualty Edition,* March 14, 1986, p. 4. Reprinted with permission.
5. Colleen Mulcahy, "Hunter Fuels Tort Reform Debate in Ill.," *National Underwriter, Property & Casualty Edition,* March 21, 1986, p. 6. Reprinted with permission.
6. Irvin Molotsky, "Drive to Limit Product Liability Awards Grows as Consumer Groups Object," *The New York Times,* March 2, 1986, p. 20. Copyright © 1986 by The New York Times Company. Reprinted by permission.
7. "Sorry, Your Policy Is Cancelled," *supra* note 2, at 25.
8. Michael Brody, "When Products Turn Into Liabilities," *Fortune,* March 3, 1986, p. 23. Copyright © 1986 Time, Inc. Reprinted with permission.
9. Ibid.
10. Mulcahy, *supra* note 5, at 62.
11. Tamar Lewin, "Business and the Law: The Big Debate Over Litigation," *The New York Times,* May 13, 1986, p. D2. Copyright © 1986 by The New York Times Company. Reprinted by permission.
12. Ibid.
13. Ibid.

11. NO FAULT, NO FEE

1. Tom Dunkel, "Battle for the Bucks," *New Jersey Monthly,* November 1984, p. 76. Copyright © 1984 by Aylesworth Communications Corp. Reprinted with permission.
2. "Whatever Happened to No-Fault," *Consumer Reports,* September 1984, p. 511–13, 546.
3. For information on operation and cost of no-fault auto insurance, see *Compensating Auto Accident Victims: A Follow-up Report on No-Fault Auto Insurance Experiences* (Washington, D.C.: U.S. Department of Transportation, May 1985); Jeffrey O'Connell and Peter Spiro, "Whatever Happened to No-Fault?," *The Washington Monthly,* April 1986, pp. 33–37.

4. See Jeffrey O'Connell and Robert Joost, "Giving Motorists a Choice Between Fault and No-Fault Insurance," *Virginia Law Review* 72 (February 1986): 61–89.

12. NEO-NO-FAULT

1. L. Burchard, "Newsletter: Social Sciences." Reprinted by permission from *Psychiatric News*, Vol. 8, no. 1, p. 6. Copyright © by the American Psychiatric Association.
2. Stephen Wermiel, "Injured Athletes Face Dilemma: Cash or Court?," *The Wall Street Journal*, March 22, 1985, p. 27. Reprinted by permission of *The Wall Street Journal*. © Dow Jones & Company, Inc., 1985. All Rights Reserved.
3. P.S. Atiyah, "No Fault Compensation: A Question That Will Not Go Away." *Tulane Law Review* 54 (February 1980): 291–93. Copyright ©1980 by Tulane Law Review Association. Reprinted with permission.
4. The ideas for tort reform in this chapter are drawn from the following legal scholarship: Jeffrey O'Connell, "Offers That Can't Be Refused: Foreclosure of Personal Injury Claims by Defendants' Prompt Tender of Claimants' Net Economic Losses," *Northwestern University Law Review* 77(December 1982): 589–632; Henson Moore and Jeffrey O'Connell, "Foreclosing Medical Malpractice Claims by Prompt Tender of Economic Loss," *Louisiana Law Review* 44(1984): 1267–87; Jeffrey O'Connell, "A 'Neo-No-Fault' Contract in Lieu of Tort: Preaccident Guarantee of Postaccident Settlement Offers," *California Law Review* 73(May 1985): 898–916; Jeffrey O'Connell, "Alternatives to the Tort System for Personal Injury," *San Diego Law Review* 23(January–February 1986): 17–35.

APPENDIX

1. Jeffrey O'Connell, "Neo No-Fault Remedies for Medical Injuries: Coordinated Statutory and Contractual Alternatives," *Law and Contemporary Problems* 49 (1986) No. 2.

Index

"Accident brokers," 68
"Add-on" states, 116
Adversary system, 32, 37
Advisory Commission on
 Intergovernmental Relations, 75
Advisory Committee on Immunization
 Practice (ACIP), 101, 102, 105
Agent Orange case, 13–14, 16–21
AIDS, 105, 110
Airplane crash cases, 38
Alexander, Fred C., Jr., 45
Allstate Insurance Company, 59, 111
Ambulance chasers, 57–59, 68–69
American Airlines crash, 57, 69
American Bar Association Journal, 24
American College of Obstetricians and
 Gynecologists, 87, 88, 89
American Cyanamid Co., 100, 101–105
American Lawyer, The, 61
American Medical Association, 39, 89
American Telephone and Telegraph
 Company (AT&T), 24, 29
Angoff, Jay, 82, 108–109
Arkansas, 93
Asbestos cases, 73, 79, 97–100, 110, 111
Ashbury, William C., 81
Association of Trial Lawyers of America
 (ATLA), 108, 117
Athletic insurance contracts, 137–138
Atiyah, Patrick, 139
Atomic tests, 78
Attorneys Devoted to Ohio People
 Totally (ADOPT), 117–118
Austin, Jerry, 81–82
Automobile accident cases, 32, 43–45,
 52–54, 111; and ambulance chasers,
 57–59, 68–69; and eyewitness
 testimony, 25–27; and no-fault
 insurance, 113–122
Automobile insurance premiums, 118,
 119, 120

Bailey, F. Lee, 23
Baptist Medical Center (Brooklyn), 110
Barnett, Ralph L., 36
Barse, Joseph, 52
Batenger, Dr. (Sweden), 102
Bay St. Louis, Mo., 76
"Bedpan" insurance co-ops, 89, 90–91,
 111
Bell Helmets, 44, 45
Bendectin, 94
Berentson, Jane, 61–64
Bergman, Melvin, 41
Beverly, Diane, 80
Birth defect cases, 94
Birthing Center of Delaware, 85
Bismarck, Prince von, 127
Bleecher, Maxwell M., 28, 30
Boise, David, 28–29, 30
Brady, Bruce, 47
Bray, Robert M., 25
Brodeur, Paul, 97–100, 110
Brunswick County, Va., 81
Burgeon, Judee K., 27
Business Roundtable, 110
Butler, Dennis and Charles, 43

Cahn, Elliot, 24
California, 108; Insurance Department,
 59
California Computer Products Inc., 28
California League of Cities, 76
Cancer deaths, 78, 79
Cap mechanism, 135
Caroline County, Va., 81
Carroll, William J., 76
Catastrophic injury, 137–138
Chamberlain, Terry N., 41
Chastain, James, 80
Chesley, Stanley, 18
Chicago Police Department, 59
Chicago Sun-Times, 57–59, 64–69

Children, sexual abuse of, 75, 80
"Claims-made" policy, 91
Class action suits, 13, 78, 111
Claybrook, Joan, 108
Coalition of Consumer Justice, 108
Cogen, Joel, 77
Colleges, 79
Colley, Michael F., 34
Common law, 109, 118, 119–120
Comparative negligence law, 49–50
Congress Watch, 82
Connecticut Conference of Municipalities, 77
Connell, Shirley, 89
Consolidated Edison, 62–63
Consumer groups, 108, 112, 119
Consumer Reports, 115
Consumers Union, 119
Contingent fees, 71, 107, 118
Contributory negligence, 50–51
Corboy, Philip, 31–32, 39–40
Courie, Maurice N., 86
"Creative" law, 82
Crown, David, 38

Dade County, Fla., 93
Dalkon Shield, 73, 110
Danforth, John, 135
Day-care centers, 80–81, 109
Defendants' characteristics, 25
"Defensive medicine," 88, 89–90
Demichelis, Robert, 115, 119
Deterrent behavior, 134
DiGrazia, Robert J., 33
Discovery proceedings, 99
District of Columbia, 52–54, 75, 119 120, 121
Doctors: dishonesty, 65–66, 71; income, 87
Dooley, Jim, 128
Dow, Merrell, 94
DPT vaccine, 105
Dukakis, Michael, 135
Dunkel, Tom, 113–114
DuPont Company, 83

Ediger, Jerry, 138
Electric Accident Investigation Handbook, The (Mazer), 38
Emotional injury case, 41–42
Encoding, 26

Expert testimony, 33–42
Eyewitness testimony, 25–27

Failure Analysis Associates, 110
Falik, Milton, 45–49
Farrell, Jimmy, 14, 15
Federal Communications Commission, 24
Federal government as defendant, 77–79
Feinberg, Kenneth R., 16, 17, 18
Fiksel, Joseph, 82
Fine, Roger, 94
Fiore, Joseph, 77
Fisher, Richard L., 81
Florida, 87, 90, 116, 119, 133–134
FMC Corporation, 82, 110
Football, 1–12, 81, 137–138
Foran, John F., 76
Ford Motor Corporation, 99
Forgery cases, 38
Fortune magazine, 97, 110
Frazza, George, 94
Fredericksburg, Va., 81

Galanter, Marc, 111
Gallup poll, 61
Garcia, Roy, 76
Garment, Leonard, 16, 17, 18
General Accounting Office, 109, 111–112
Georgetown University Hospital, 53
Gephardt, Richard, 135
Germany, 127
Gettinger, Stephen A., 87
Glynn, Faith Ann, 115, 117
Godosky, Richard, 50
Goldin, Harrison, 77
Gonda, Judith, 29, 30
Goodale, James C., 74
Graham, Timothy, 93
Great Britain, 127
Green, Joyce Hens, 35
Greer, Timothy A., 77
Grossman, Alissa, Marjorie, and David, 45–49
Gym class accident case, 50–52

Habush, Robert, 108
Hacker, Andrew, 97–100
Hahnemann Medical School, 34
Hallisey, Robert J., 36
Hamden, Conn., 76
Hannon, Joseph M., 53

Harlem Hospital Center, 110
Harrison, Michael and Carol, 50–52
Hart, Gary, 100
Hartford Insurance Company, 7
Hearst, Patty, 23
Helicopter rotors, 82–83
Herbert, A.P., 103
Higginbotham, Patrick E., 35–36, 37
Hillcrest General Hospital (Queens, N.Y.), 46, 47
Hinckley, John W., Jr., 36
Hit-and-run vehicles, 122
Hood College (Frederick, Md.), 79
Hospitals: dishonesty, 66–68; safety, 110
Huber, Peter, 101
Hunter, J. Robert, 108, 109, 111, 119

Ice skating rinks, 74
Illinois, 90, 115
Indiana, 108
Industrial Insurance Management Corporation, 81
Insurance: fraud, 58–72 *passim*; industry, 108–109, 111, 112; payments, 107, 126, 130
Insurance Information Institute, 80
International Business Machines, 28–29

Jackson Township, N.J., 77
Jenkins, John A., 37, 39
Johns Hopkins University, 34
Johns Manville, 73, 79, 97–100
Johnson (Emil) *v. American Cyanamid Co.*, 100–105
Johnson, Robert, 95
Johnson & Johnson, 93–94
"Joint and several liability," 107–108
Jolley, Helen and Sheldon, 78
Judges: bias, 30–31; dishonesty, 70, 71; immunity, 134–135
Juries, 23–32
Jury Verdict Research, Inc., 82

Kalmowitz, Gail, 14–15
Kansas Supreme Court, 104
Kaplan, Lawrence I., 35
Kaplan, Martin F., 27–28
Katzenbach, Nicholas, 28
Keiser, Lester, 133–134
Kerr, Norbert L., 25
Kings County, N.Y., Hospital Center, 110

Kitch, Edmund, 100–105
KNBC-TV (Los Angeles), 59–61
Korean Air Lines downing, 38
Krohley, William, 20

Ladder accident case, 40–41
Lader, Spencer, 70–71
Lederer, John and Maryann, 68–69
Lederle Laboratories, 95, 101–104
Liability insurance, 73–83
Litigation Sciences, 29
Little, Arthur D., 82
Lloyds of London, 109
Lobster fishermen's drowning case, 77–78
Loring, Theodore, 86
Los Angeles, Calif., 76
Luken, Thomas, 108
Lurito, Richard, 45

McBroom, Doug, 1–12, 137, 138
McCann, John, 80
McClure, Hugh, 7, 9
McCormick, Paul V., 51
McDaniel, L. Robert, 81
McDermott, Francis M., 38
McDonnell, Edmund J., 39
McKenna, Jeremiah, 70, 71
McKinney, John A., 99
Malott, Robert H., 110
Manhattan's Sky Rink, 74
Manke, H.I., 76
Manville Corporation, 73, 79, 97–100
Maryland, 116
Mass disaster litigation, 78
Massachusetts, 91, 120, 135
Mazer, William, 37–38
MCI Communications Corporation, 24, 29
Mecklenburg County, Va., 82
Medical Liability Mutual Insurance Company (MLMIC), 89, 90
Medical malpractice, 14–16, 34, 45–49, 70, 85–95, 110, 128–129
Mega, Christopher, 71
Memory, 26
Menninger Foundation, 43
Michigan, 90, 115, 116–117
Midwives, 85
Miller, Bob, 111
Miller, George, 80
Miller, Gerald R., 27

Ministers, 74
Minnesota, 116
Missouri, 108
Mixson, William T., 88–89
Mock juries, 24, 27
Molokai, Hawaii, 85
Montessori schools, 75
Montrose, Colo., 77
Moore, Henson, 135
Morning sickness drug, 94
Moynihan, Pat, 136
Municipal liability, 75–77
Mutual insurance companies, 89, 90–91, 111

Nader, Ralph, 108, 109, 119
Nardi, Joseph, 92, 93
National Academy of Sciences, 102
National Center for State Courts, 35, 37, 111
National Federation of High School Athletic Associations, 137
National Insurance Consumer Organization, 108, 119
National Law Journal, 17, 18, 19–20
National Underwriter, 29, 59
National Weather Services (NWS), 77–78
Neo-no-fault insurance, 130–138; legislation and contracts compared, 141–144
Net economic loss, 130–133
Nevada, 120
New Hampshire, 91
New Jersey, 50–51, 77, 113, 116
New Jersey AIR (Automobile Insurance Reform), 114
New Jersey Monthly, 113
New Mexico, 91
New Republic, 74
New York City, 77, 110; Transit Authority, 49–50
New York Court of Appeals, 37
New York State: comparative negligence law, 49–50; Health Department, 110; malpractice insurance, 86–87, 88, 89, 90, 91; no-fault insurance, 116, 117; Senate Committee on Crime and Corrections, 70–71
New York State Medical Society, 87
New York Times, 14, 16, 34, 45, 46, 48, 49–50, 70, 73–74, 77, 87–88, 89, 94
New York Times Magazine, 35, 37
New Yorker, 97
Newport Beach, Calif., 74
Newsweek, 73, 90
No-fault insurance, 113–122. *See also* Neo-no-fault insurance
"No-lawsuit" states, 116
Norfolk, Va., 81

Obstetricians, 85–89
"Occurrence" policy, 91
O'Hare Airport crash, 57, 69
Oliver, Charlie, 51
Olson, Lyndon, 111
Orange, Calif., 80
Oregon, 116
Ortho-Gynol, 94
Outrageous Misconduct: The Asbestos Industry on Trial (Brodeur), 97–100

"Pain and Suffering" awards, 107, 114, 115, 116, 118, 119, 124–125, 135
Pegalis, Steven, 46–47, 48–49
Pennsylvania, 120
Perceptual judgment, 26
Pertussis vaccine, 105
Pharmaceuticals companies, 73, 74, 93–95; *Johnson v. American Cyanamid Co.*, 100–105
Plaster of paris burn cases, 93–94
Policeman, paralyzed, case, 76
Polio vaccines, 101–105
Political system, 118
Power-tool injury case, 39–40
Pre-school Association of California, 80–81
Premature baby cases, 14–16
Product Liability Alliance, 82
Product liability cases, 34, 44–45 82–83, 97–105, 110, 111, 129
Professional Insurance Agents of Connecticut, 77
Psychology of the Courtroom, The (Kerr and Bray), 25, 30–31
Public opinion pollsters, 29
Punitive damages, 103, 107, 134

Quam, Paul, 4, 7, 8

Index

Racial bias, 25, 31
Raspberry, William, 43
Reagan administration, 108, 130
Real estate brokers, 74
Recall, 26–27
Redding, Calif., school system, 74
Referral fees, 57–58, 71
Regulation magazine, 100
Reid, Inez Smith, 75
Renton, Wash., School District, 2, 3
Rhode Island, 91
"Right to sue," 109, 118, 119–120
Roanoke County, Va., 81
Robins, A.H., 73, 110
Robinson, Judith, 79
Rogers, Kenny, 99
Ronk, David A., 86
Ruby, W.J., 99
Ruedlinger, Doug, 137
Rusk Institute, 53

Sabin vaccine, 101–105
Safety helmet manufacturers, 2, 3, 44, 73
St. Paul Fire and Marine Insurance Company, 91–93
Saks, Michael J., 37
Sales, Bruce, 34–35
Salk, Daryl and Jonas, 102
Salk vaccine, 101–105
Scalettar, Raymond, 39
Schindler, Norman, 92
Schmutz, John F., 83
School burglar liability case, 74
School insurance contracts, 137–138
School liability cases, 74, 75, 81–82
Schroeter, Leonard, 5, 6, 8–9, 10
Schwartz, Victor, 78, 79, 82
Schwarz, Richard H., 86, 90
Scituate, Mass., 75
Seattle, Wash., School District, 2, 137
Seattle Times, 10
Self-insurance, 95
Settlements, 13–21
"Shadow jury," 28–29
Shapiro, David, 16, 17, 18
Shellan, Gerard, 8
Schultz, Charles, 74
Silfen, Thomas E., 41–42
South Tucson, Ariz., 76
Sovereign immunity, 76

Spencer, Gerry, 109
Spermicidal cream, 94
Spotsylvania County, Va., 81
Starks, David G., 110
State University of New York's Downstate Medical Center (Brooklyn), 86, 90
States' rights, 108
Stein, Jacob A., 51
Stein, Andrew J., 110
Stephens, Milo, 49–50
Strausz, Ivan K., 87–88, 90, 95
Strict liability, 107
Stump v. Sparkman, 134
Subway case, 49–50
Swimming accident cases, 74–75
"Swoop and squat" maneuver, 60

Terranova, Charles W., 75
Texas, 116; Board of Insurance, 111
Thompson, Chris and Louisa Ann ("Lou"), 1–12, 137, 138
Thompson, Robert, 60–61
Thomson, James M., 81
Threshold requirements, 116, 119, 120
Tiernan, Patricia, 44, 45
Time magazine, 73
Todd, James S., 89
Tomeo, Joseph, 114
Tort liability system, 54–55, 73, 97, 99, 100, 125–126
Tort reform, 107–112, 139
Tortfeasor, 124–125
Towse, Virginia, 3, 4, 5, 7, 8, 10
Toxic-exposure cases, 78–79
Toxic waste case, 77
Transaction costs, 127
Trial lawyers, 108, 109, 110, 112, 117–118, 135–136
Truck wheel rims, multipiece, cases, 110
Tullock, Gordon, 99
20th Century Insurance, 60–61

Uninsured motorists (UM) insurance, 122
United States Congress, 135
United States Department of Transportation, 117, 120
United States House of Representatives Select Committee on Children, Youth and Family, 80

United States Justice Department, 18, 78–79, 111, 112
United States Supreme Court, 134
University of Arizona, 34
University of Hawaii Medical Center, 85
University of Maryland, 34
University of Nebraska, 34
U.S. News & World Report, 73, 79
USA Today, 73

Vaccine cases, 74, 95, 101–105, 134
Vance, Wayne, 78
Van Duizend, Richard, 37
Van Gessel, Fritz A., 46, 47
"Verbal" thresholds, 116, 117, 120
Veterans Administration, 18
Vietnam War veterans, 13–14, 16–21
Villanova University, 34
Vinson, David E., 28, 29
Virginia school insurance, 81–82

Wall Street Journal, 28, 30, 73, 78, 79
Wapanucka, Okla., 76

Washington Interscholastic Athletic Association (WIAA), 2, 4–5
Washington Post, 33, 34, 39, 43, 50, 51, 73
Watts, Cory, Cordelia, and Roy, 43–45
Weaver, Jean, 80
Weeda, Philip, Helen, and David, 52–54
Wehbe, Debbie, 80
Weinstein, Jack B., 13–14, 16–21
Weinstein, Jeremy S., 71
Weitz, Harvey, 35
Whooping cough vaccine, 95
Wildman, Max, 32
Willard, Richard, 78–79
Willmore, Robert, 111, 112
Wittman, Marty, 138
WLS-TV (Chicago), 59, 64, 66
Wonnell, Edith, 85
Workers' compensation, 120, 127–128

Yannacone, Victor J., Jr., 18
Younger, Irving, 34, 36
YWCA (Baltimore), 80

Zeizel, Hans, 28

About the Authors

JEFFREY O'CONNELL, the John Allan Love Professor of Law at the University of Virginia Law School, specializes in accident and insurance law. He coauthored the principal work that proposed no-fault auto insurance, and he has written several other books on accident law. A graduate of Exeter Academy, Dartmouth College, and the Harvard Law School, he has been a recipient of two Guggenheim Fellowships. Since 1973 he has been on the Educational Advisory Board of the Guggenheim Foundation. He also serves on the Medical and Safety Committee of the National Collegiate Athletic Association (NCAA), and he has served on the board of directors of Consumers Union.

C. BRIAN KELLY, a lecturer in journalism at the University of Virginia, is also editor of *Military History* and *World War II* magazines. Sixteen of his twenty years as a newspaper reporter were spent at the *Washington Star*. His work there earned a number of journalism awards; he was cited as "Communicator of the Year" by the National Wildlife Federation and for public affairs reporting by the American Political Science Association. He also was awarded a study/writing fellowship by the APSA. He contributed a chapter to the book *Who's Poisoning America*, by Ralph Nader et al. (Sierra Clubs Books, 1981), and has published fiction and nonfiction in a number of magazines, among them *Yankee* and *Reader's Digest*. He is a graduate of The Hill School and Yale University.